JUDSON CORNWALL

"Disciple is not a dangerous word, for Jesus discipled men unto maturity. In his book, Bill Ligon first walks us through the pages of church history showing us the excesses past generations have come into in their discipleship programs, and then he takes us to the Sermon on the Mount to see Christ's principles of discipling men.

"Mr. Ligon has done his homework well and has given us a book that is enlightening, challenging, and quite comprehensive. My copy will be well marked and will remain in my personal library for a long time to come. I heartily recommend it to anyone who is more than casually interested in discipleship."

GERALD DERSTINE

"Bill is a qualified man to give answers to some of the subtle heresies stymying the move of God. You will sense a spirit of humility and concern coming from the heart of the author."

KEN SUMRALL

"The reader can be assured that the author of this book is neither writing defensively nor out of his own hurts. He is attempting to express the feelings of hundreds of God's little sheep and undershepherds who have bled and are now bleeding through the extremes of discipleship methods.

"In order to bring genuine unity to the Body of Christ, we must not simply allow sores to scab over. Rather, we must allow the Holy Spirit to use us to operate, fully exposing and bringing healing to the infected parts. This, I believe, has been aptly and kindly done in this book by a man with a pastor's heart—Bill Ligon."

DR. C.M. WARD

"This volume is long overdue. It is a discipline for believers found in straightforward, understandable Bible teaching. I strongly advise the study of these chapters."

DISCIPLESHIP:
The Jesus View

DISCIPLESHIP: The Jesus View

(An Alternative to Extremism)

by
BILL LIGON
with
ROBERT PAUL LAMB

Logos International
Plainfield, New Jersey

Unless noted as NASB (New American
Standard Bible) all Scripture quota-
tions are taken from the King James
Version of the Bible.

"I go to prepare a
place for you."
(John 14:2)
—Jesus Christ

To:

The body of Christ,
to encourage healing for you.

Table of Contents

Preface

Jesus Christ prayed to the Father, "I in them, and Thou in Me, that they may be perfected in unity, that the world may know that Thou didst send Me, and didst love them, even as Thou didst love Me" (John 17:23 NASB).

The apostle Paul continued the call for Christian unity—doing so to every church to which he addressed himself. To the Philippian church, he wrote, "Only conduct yourselves in a manner worthy of the gospel of Christ; so that whether I come and see you or remain absent, I may hear of you that you are standing firm in one spirit, with one mind striving together for the faith of the gospel" (Phil. 1:27 NASB).

The prayer of Jesus and the exhortation of Paul are yet to be fulfilled with lasting effect in the body of Christ. Of course, there have always been disciples committed to the Lord to perfect His unity in their hearts. They are found throughout the pages of Church history bravely calling for balance and unity with the body.

Their commitments to fellow Christians have allowed a freedom where the disciple's supreme allegiance to the Lord Jesus Christ could be respected. I believe it is just such freedom in discipleship which allows the Holy Spirit to bring to fulfillment the wishes of Jesus expressed in His prayer in John 17:23.

The Lord placed a burden upon me to write this book to encourage freedom, unity and balance in the body of Christ. Balanced teaching on biblical principles encourages healing; unity is restored.

Each time God has moved sovereignly down through Church history to restore the Church's vitality, men's hopes for permanent restoration have been stirred. Such was the case for me when my family and I were baptized in the Holy Spirit in 1971, while serving as Southern Baptist missionaries in our adopted country of Spain.

I was confident that anyone who experienced the same renewing presence of the Holy Spirit would gather in a glorious restoration of the body of Christ. All evidence suggested a final ingathering and restoration of the Church as one body "of the same mind, maintaining the same love, united in spirit, intent on one purpose" (Phil. 2:2 NASB). I knew the purpose was for Christ's sake.

Yet, after several years of restoration, sincere Bible teachers moved internationally to bring the renewal movement into orderly authority. Unfortunately, their deliberate and rapid move to establish authority fractured areas of the charismatic revival.

Taking the word "discipleship" to describe their work of bringing men into mature Christian character, these teachers created a controversy in the body of Christ. The word "discipleship" enraged some who resented the word's use to identify a specific organization's primary thrust. The word "discipleship" was lost to many others, who, for conscience's sake, could not agree with their brothers' emphasis.

In this book, I am making a distinction between the words "shepherdship" and "discipleship." I use the term "shepherdship" to describe the work of teachers who called disciples into one-to-one submission sealing men to men. Such efforts in recent years have led to the formation of a new discipleship effort, where the basis for church government is one-to-one submission of a sheep to his shepherd. Such unilateral submission to the authority of one man has led to numerous abuses.

I am personally calling for the word "discipleship" to be liberated and recovered for use by all parts of the body of Christ.

Discipleship is short-term and often intensive in character. It is not for everyone in the body of Christ all the time. Balanced discipleship brings the disciple into maturity without violating the sovereign relationship Jesus Christ has with him.

Shepherdship is a long-term and less intensive relationship between undershepherds and the sheep. The beautiful shepherd-sheep analogy need not be lost within the body of Christ. Pastors and members can speak in those terms without invading the sovereign authority of the "Great Shepherd" over all the members of His flock.

When I saw division coming in the renewal movement, I felt led to reevalute the teachings of Jesus to His disciples. I saw men were overemphasizing the method Jesus used to the detriment of the Word He taught them.

The words Jesus spoke have Spirit and Life in them. They produce maturity in the disciple. I believe emphasizing *what* Jesus taught as opposed to *how* He taught will bring healing to the body of Christ.

I owe a great debt to my co-author, Robert Paul Lamb, who has diligently followed after my work, guiding the formation of this book into its present form.

I want to particularly thank Jamie Buckingham, Gerald Derstine, Ken Sumrall and Dr. C. M. Ward for reading the manuscript and making helpful suggestions, although I make it plain they are not responsible for my conclusions.

My co-pastor, Calder Kinney, and church treasurer and fellow elder, George W. Counts, Jr., also read the manuscript and gave meaningful suggestions in the light of our five years' experience in overseeing a renewal church together. I am grateful for their help and encouragement.

My dear wife, Dorothy Jean, and our sons, William and John, have encouraged me to dedicate the time necessary to complete the book. No one could be more blessed than I to have my family support the work so strongly.

Most of all, I want to thank our Lord for what I consider a very timely anointing to write my first book.

I point out to the reader that chapters three and four are not intended to be exhaustive chapters of detailed Church history. I only give a cursory review of some events in history to focus upon repeated problems in the area of discipleship. Readers desiring a complete historical study should at least read the works of those authors referred to in the footnotes of the book.

Names and places in my personal testimony are fictitious when such changes have been considered in the best interest of the persons concerned.

Bill Ligon
Brunswick, Georgia

Foreword

Every genuine Christian movement has begun with extremism.

When a clock pendulum has hung motionless for a long time, it takes a big push to get it started. A little nudge won't do it. Even if the pendulum is only supposed to move in a six-inch arc, it will probably take a twelve-inch push to get it started. Eventually, if the clock is level, the gears oiled and the hands not frozen in place, the pendulum will find its proper arc and begin tick-tocking at the correct pace.

What I am saying is I do not reject nor react to initial extremes—in clocks or the Kingdom. They are necessary to get us in motion.

The problem arises when someone comes along and thinks he has to keep pushing the pendulum—that big arcs are better than small ones—and is unwilling to let the wound spring of the Holy Spirit exert just the right pressure to keep the thing on time.

Or, equally bad, some frightened person, afraid the pendulum will swing in wider and wider arcs rather than finding its own pace, will grab it and try to stop it completely.

Either way you have big problems—especially if it is God's time for the clock to begin running again.

I personally believe it is God's time for the clock of discipleship to begin ticking once again. When I worked with Juan Carlos Ortiz on *Call to Discipleship* in the mid-seventies I realized I was helping set the long-motionless pendulum of discipleship into motion.

At that time the concepts of the Argentine pastor were viewed as extreme. To counter this, Dan Malachuk, the publisher, and I both wrote forewords in the book, warning the readers to go slow. One push was enough for a while.

Dan said: "Because the ideas of this book are so fresh and stimulating, we are all in danger of going overboard in our response to them. We will be tempted to try to duplicate what happened in Argentina by slavish imitation. Let us steadfastly resist such temptation."

I wrote: "Some will read this book and use it as a mechanic's manual, a sort of program plan book for the kingdom. It is these I fear. This is not a book of methods, it is a book of principles. . . . May God deliver us from those who are unwilling to arrive at their own conclusions through prayer, fasting and waiting on the Lord."

However, I have long suspected most book readers do not pay any attention to forewords and prefaces. Therefore, I realized that despite all warnings, I was helping set the old pendulum of discipleship, which had hung on dead center for many years, once again swinging.

At the same time, outstanding Bible teachers from Christian Growth Ministries in Ft. Lauderdale, Florida, were daring to give expression to the impression they said God had put into their hearts. As they saw it, preaching was for proclamation, discipleship was for application. In bold, daring moves, they began to put into practice methods which they expected would call men to account for their professed loves—the love of God and the love of the body of Christ. Taking a page from the book of their Catholic cousins, they began calling the men for whom they felt accountable into orders of covenant relationship.

It was an extreme shove of the pendulum Ortiz had set into motion. I am convinced, however, that despite all their mistakes (and they have been legion), it was necessary to get us off dead center.

Immediately two things happened. A number of men, thinking the old clock was getting ready to leap off the wall and crash to the floor, grabbed the pendulum (and the pendulum pushers) and tried to bring it to a stop. Other young Christians, excited over the new motion and the new sense of power which was theirs in authority, jumped in and gave the old thing additional hefty shoves. In many areas the pushers were stronger than the stoppers and instead of allowing the pendulum to find its own arc, with a normal tick-tock, the old clock began to sound like TICK-TOCK-TOCKETY-TOCK-GET-OUT-OF-MY-WAY-HERE-COMES-ULTIMATE-TRUTH.

Just as the rebellion of the peasants was the natural but unfortunate outcome of Luther's reformation, so we have had our share of extremes as the discipleship clock has begun to run. Luther, the extremist, did share the responsibility of the peasant rebellion—even though he deplored it. It took generations of healing and correction to bring balance to the radicalism of the Reformation; just as it will take time to overcome the extremism and havoc brought by this new movement. Although the blame for rocking the charismatic ship may rest with a few, some of us feared that ship was slowly becoming dead in the water and was in danger of being sucked into the humanism of the cultural church.

I am not of that school. I have an overpowering sense of the ability of God to guide and protect His sheep. "Those who come to me I will in no wise cast out." Those who fear that extreme man can pluck the lambs out of God's hand simply don't have a very big view of God.

On the other hand, there have been many undue extremes which need to be corrected. In some areas men have replaced "the Lord is my Shepherd" with "the shepherd is my Lord." What is needed is a sense of history as well as a knowledge of the Bible.

I believe this book helps bring that balanced perspective to the Kingdom.

I have known Bill Ligon for a number of years. While he was a Southern Baptist missionary to Spain he received the fullness of the Holy Spirit. Later he returned to the States and accepted the call to the large and prestigious First Baptist Church of Brunswick, Georgia. When it became obvious the church was rejecting him because of his spiritual emphasis, he and his associate pastor quietly resigned rather than cause a split.

Now Bill is giving apostolic leadership to a growing number of people in the island area of Georgia's coast. When, after some sad encounters with men involved in extreme discipleship, he felt compelled to write this book, I challenged him to keep it positive, to give us perspective of history, to help us see that across the centuries men have endeavored to make disciples, to help us learn from their errors, their discoveries—and most of all to help us see the Jesus view of discipleship.

Working closely with Robert Paul Lamb, and always consulting with men with balanced ministries in the Kingdom, Bill has come forth with a magnificent book, presenting an alternative to extremism.

Yet, even as I applaud him for this book, I also applaud the men who have been willing to set the pendulum in motion. The charismatic clock, it seems, has been pointing to five minutes after nine o'clock in the morning ever since the movement got underway in 1960. Now the pendulum is swinging again, set in motion—whether we like it or not—by those who dare to die for what they believe. They have acted, and set the old clock rocking so hard it's almost ready to fall off the mantle. This book is not written to stop the motion. It is written as a call for balance—allowing the Holy Spirit to once again do that which he does best, bring to mind all the things Jesus taught us.

Who, if you recall, was something of an extremist himself.

Jamie Buckingham
Melbourne, Florida

DISCIPLESHIP:
The Jesus View

1 | *Seeds of Division*

I never intended to pastor a "charismatic" congregation. In fact, that was the last thing in my mind when my wife, our two sons and I returned from six years in Spain as Southern Baptist missionaries. Although God had sovereignly baptized us in the Holy Spirit while we were in Spain, I clearly intended to work within my denomination to bring renewal.

But that was not to be. Two years after returning to the States, I found myself embroiled in a heated controversy as pastor of the First Baptist Church of Brunswick, Georgia. My charismatic beliefs—that the supernatural gifts of the Holy Spirit listed in 1 Corinthians 12 should operate in public worship today—were called into question by a small faction in the church.

After the issues had been pressed several times without success, rather than split the church I resigned, along with Frank Patterson who at the time was one of my assistants. Frank was a capable young minister with a bright future. I had no idea where we would go or what we would do. I simply felt we should "sit tight" and wait on God. Frank wanted to leave town immediately, but I was able to persuade him to wait to see what God was doing.

In a matter of weeks, a group of people—some who had been at First Baptist and others who had been in the renewal movement for years—were gathering around us with one fervent request. "Pastor us," they begged. "Let's have a charismatic church here where the gifts of the Holy Spirit can be manifested as they were in the primitive church."

"Could this be the Lord?" I asked myself. In a short time, I would know.

Our first meeting was in the civic room of a bank on St. Simons Island, just across the river from Brunswick. A hundred people showed up. We quickly moved to the larger quarters of the city recreation building as word spread about our services. It seemed as if all of southeast Georgia was abuzz about the charismatic activities in Brunswick.

Within months, the crowds were averaging 200 to 300 per service. We had a full-blown congregation on our hands—charitable, Christ-loving, hand-waving, miracle-believing, tongues-speaking charismatics. Church would never be the same. They were so eager to hear the Word of God taught, I found a new excitement in pastoring which some of my colleagues in other churches said they were missing.

It was natural that I should give the major leadership, since I had done that at our former church. In addition to Frank, who was some ten years younger, we added Calder Kinney, a Methodist pastor, who joined us first on a part-time basis, then later permanently. While I took the lead in our meetings, I was also submitted to the other two as fellow elders. However, this did not satisfy Frank.

"Bill, what you need to do is submit yourself to a man outside of Brunswick," he often suggested.

"I don't understand how that'll possibly help me here," I answered. "I think the better approach is for me to open my life to the brothers in the local fellowship where I live. You and Calder know I work for mutual submission among us. You're free to correct me any time you wish. You're the people I live my Christian experience before."

"No, I don't agree," he often rebutted. "A covenant relationship with another person will bring strength into your life that you've never known before. You're plugged into God's line of authority then. You can hear more clearly from God. I could even submit to you more completely if you submitted yourself to a prominent shepherd elsewhere."

I knew where Frank was getting his ideas. Respected teachers were conducting seminars around the nation—and distributing thousands of tapes—teaching what Frank was saying. It seemed the teachings on discipleship, church government, submission and covenant relationships were planting seeds of sectarianism in the charismatic renewal.

In a sincere effort to call Christians into spiritual maturity, these Bible teachers were guiding their followers into what could be extremism of personal discipleship. I was concerned about the results.

I remembered that Brigham Young, the second President of the Mormon Church, had led men into similar extremes with his doctrine of "sealing men to men." He had introduced a ceremony where men and their wives would be adopted by a spiritual leader. The idea was to establish the kingdom of God on the earth, where counsel and guidance could be passed down to the believers. Young said he was "sealed" or submitted to Joseph Smith—even in death. Each man was submitted one-on-one to the singular authority of a man over him.

In one of his sermons, Young declared, "Those that are adopted into my family and take me for their counsellor, if I continue faithfully I will preside over them throughout all eternity and will stand at their head. . . ." Such relationships were supposed to give some kind of strength to Young's followers they couldn't receive in a direct, personal way from God.

Strength was a subject I was hearing a lot about lately. Many young pastors—some who had been suddenly thrust into pastoring new churches—were frequently coming to me for advice. Young and inexperienced, they were insecure in their work. Some experienced a haunting loneliness and wanted to draw closer to other pastors. They looked for someone to give them strength and encouragement. They saw in my twenty years of experience just such strength. They came to be encouraged. I saw that as one method of discipleship. But I also wanted to emphasize spiritual responsibility— vertical as well as horizontal.

I could not quarrel with young pastors who wanted to relate to mature men to draw strength from them. Timothy obviously had such a relationship with Paul. But any relationship which ignored scriptural balance in its structure exposed men to dangerous extremes. Today it could be shepherdship, tomorrow another movement where less responsible men ruled with unreasonable authority. Such veneration of one man's counsel and guidance I considered "cultish."

As the "new" teachings continued on discipleship, my uneasiness grew. Finally I telephoned an old friend, Jamie Buckingham, who like me had been a Southern Baptist pastor. He agreed that some of the teachings raised questions and suggested we meet with one of the "shepherdship" teachers.

The meeting at a Florida retreat center was cordial and friendly, but the teacher made it clear he felt he had "heard from God." His response to our questions was polite but determined.

"Frankly, I'm tired of 'sermon-tasters,' " he said, referring to the many people who floated from one full gospel meeting to another. "I'm going to devote my time to developing individual disciples. I want people who desire a deeper level of commitment to God."

I liked what he said. There *was* a need to get the "meeting-hoppers" grounded in a local church. But while I never doubted his motives, I had severe questions about his methods—especially his concept of submitting to shepherds out of town, and the insistence that sheep "obey" the authority of one leader.

I came away from the meeting unsettled. Something gnawed at my insides. Frank didn't react that way though. He seemed to focus upon the need for discipling individuals. The expression "deeper level of commitment" was often in his conversation. Like many other younger men, he seemed to look at commitment more idealistically. Everything was "black" or "white" with little room for practical application of biblical principles.

Shortly afterwards, Frank announced plans to leave. "I've submitted myself to James Malone in Arkansas," he said. "I believe a covenant relationship to one shepherd over my life is the method God is going to use to bring me into my place of ministry."

"I'm puzzled by one thing," I admitted.

"What's that?"

"If you devote all of your time to a handful of your disciples, what happens to the other people in the body—the widows, the orphans, the kids whose parents don't attend? What happens to them?"

"That's not my problem," he answered, shaking his head. "God told me to devote my time to a few men under me with a shepherd over me. I'm going to do it like Jesus did."

"Well, I can't walk away from all of the other people," I said. "God's given me a burden for the whole body of Christ in Brunswick. I believe God will show me how to develop leadership without abandoning some of His people."

James Malone, the man Frank was submitting to, was also a former Southern Baptist pastor. He was a gifted Bible teacher and had previously taught in one of our seminars. Calder and I decided Frank's reasons for leaving were personal. The church gave Frank and his family a gracious "farewell."

A year passed before I recognized the significance of Frank's move. It came when he returned to our area to teach. As a gesture of respect, we invited him to be a guest speaker at our fellowship of believers.

It was during this visit that the pastor from a nearby town and a prominent family from our local church submitted themselves to Frank.

Confused, I talked with the father of the local family to ask why they were leaving our fellowship of believers. Frank had told him to accept me as his pastor when he left. He only gave mechanical responses. "You're not meeting our needs." I understood that to mean I did not give daily pastoral supervision to his family.

The next afternoon Frank came by my office. "This family has entered into a submitted relationship to me," he said. "You're not meeting their needs here so they have decided to make a change."

I knew Frank had had a close relationship with this family in the past. In fact, he had introduced them to the Lord. "But since you've moved to Arkansas, how can you possibly minister to their needs now?" I asked.

"I can travel over here frequently," he responded, "and there's always the telephone."

"But, how can a shepherd tend sheep—"

Frank interrupted. "The problem is you're not meeting their needs," he said firmly. "That's the big issue. In fact, you're not even aware of some of their problems. If you had been doing your job correctly, you would have known this family's situation."

"Just a second," I interjected. "I've been concerned about this family. I've ministered to them. Fact is, I gave them more of my time than many other families. But the father wanted me to be involved in the minutest detail of his personal life. I wanted him to stand on his own feet and be a man of God."

"That's exactly what I'm talking about," Frank countered. "That man had needs you couldn't meet. He had problems in spiritual growth nobody was dealing with. That's clearly why he and his family must have what I can offer. A submitted relationship to me will solve many of their struggles. People must be plugged in to a shepherd."

The matter weighed heavily upon me as I drove home alone that night along the winding highway through the marshes of Glynn, across the Sidney Lanier Bridge and on past the Jekyll Island exit. I knew much of what Frank was saying was true. Many people were enduring their pain in a sea of loneliness. There *were* people in the local body of Christ with needs not being met. And I could understand why that family in our fellowship of believers would respond to Frank's approach. After all, he had led them to Christ.

Yet the questions continued to bother me: How can a submitted relationship work from a distance? Wasn't the New Testament concept of the church always local? Didn't the disciples of Jesus successfully develop small group meetings without using heavy, one-on-one submission principles with the believers? And terms like "plugged in." What did that mean?

I had been hearing stories about extremes of "shepherdship" all across the country. Men embracing the movement dismissed the extremes as "horror stories" not representing their work. Before, the problem was in some distant city. Now, it was at my doorstep. But it was too early to evaluate the results.

At the same time the family from our fellowship joined Frank, the pastor of another church in a nearby town also submitted himself to him. Frank had frequently taught in the other church. Once again, I could see where his approach would appeal to others in spite of extremes inherent in the methods.

I was hearing much the same story from all over the country. Shepherdship teaching—that believers "absolutely must" be submitted to a shepherd—seemed to be producing as much fear and condemnation as it was helping others find security. Disciples were also being drawn from local fellowships and churches into shepherdship groups. Leaders and active members of Full Gospel Business Men's Fellowship International chapters abruptly "dropped out." Aglow chapters closed over the question of proper "covering" for women.

A confused couple came to me saying their son, a college freshman, had just announced he would not need their parental supervision any longer. He would now get it from his shepherd, one of his college professors.

On another occasion, a university professor from another state telephoned. Although he had known me only as a Baptist pastor, he hoped I might know what was happening among some people in his town who called themselves "charismatics."

"Some of our students who attend a particular church in town are dropping out of school," he said, a bewildered tone in his voice. "Their shepherd tells them they don't need any more education now. They've got to get ready for the end times. They seem to blindly follow his advice."

"That's foolish," I said. "They certainly don't represent the balanced charismatics I know."

"I know," he agreed, "but they say they have to do what their shepherd says if they are going to learn to hear from God."

After I hung up the phone, I wondered. "Can't the sheep hear from God praying alone or with a group of believers? In fact, isn't the shepherd a sheep, too?"

I couldn't understand the maze of situations I continually encountered. I knew of several situations where men in shepherdship seemed to have a healthy relationship with their disciples. Although there was one-to-one submission, the shepherd didn't seem so demanding in those instances.

Then it happened. I was shocked into an understanding of the problem through an experience. I had been invited to speak at a FGBMFI seminar in a south Georgia town. I had previously pastored a large church there and the chapter officers knew me and my work.

Yet the first seminar session was oppressive. The air was tense with confusion. I felt great resistance as I attempted to teach. Finally I stopped, admitted my problem to the people and prayed. Everyone joined with me and the heaviness gradually lifted. The session ended victoriously.

Afterwards, I was driven to my night's lodging by the chapter president. "I'm sorry for what happened tonight," he said apologetically. "When we arrived for the meeting, brothers from a local church called a 'submitted body' confronted us before the meeting started. They said they had been raised up as elders over the body of Christ in this town. They claimed responsibility for any teaching the Christians in our town receive. They said you weren't submitted to anyone in the country through their chain of authority so you didn't have a right to teach here."

"I can't believe that," I said in amazement. "I'm submitted to my brothers in the body of Christ at Brunswick. We are all submitted to each other. They sent me here. In fact, I'm submitted to you men while I'm here teaching your people."

He nodded his head in agreement. "I know that. I've known your record for the last twenty years. I refused to listen to their nonsense."

"I'm glad of that," I smiled.

"They did create some problem which you recognized, though. They were sitting on the front row during the teaching. I'm sure that was the resistance everybody was feeling in the meeting."

Seeds of division had been planted in the charismatic movement. Yet at times I wondered if I had missed God. Could I have missed a biblical truth right under my nose? Had these men of sincere beliefs found "the way" to God?

I had struggled with the concepts of shepherdship for a long time, simply feeling uneasy about what I was hearing. But now the time had come for me to get some basic answers from God. I had to take a long, hard look at the entire picture of what being a disciple of Jesus meant.

I knew the Greek word for disciple was *mathetes*. There was nothing dark or mysterious about the word. It simply meant "learner." Any person could have a disciple or pupil. That was nothing new.

A brief look at the New Testament revealed something about pastors having their own disciples which I hadn't noticed before. The word disciple did not appear in Scripture after Acts 21. Peter, James, John and Paul never referred to any person as "my disciple." In fact, I couldn't find a place where they used the word in their writings. They called Christians by several affectionate names like "brethren," "beloved," "saints," and "my little children."

I knew somehow I was in for an exhaustive look for the

truth. It would not be accomplished easily. Yet since I had been a young boy growing up in a rural Baptist church in Alabama, I knew God would respond to a sincere heart turned towards Him. This time that truth would be put to a severe test.

2 | *In Search of a Place*

In search of the truth—besides closely examining Scripture—I knew I had to look at my own life. I had been a Baptist since birth. My parents had taken me to church when I was two weeks old and I never left it. My father had been a Baptist deacon. I had received a call to the ministry in the Baptist church. I always felt I'd be a Southern Baptist pastor. That seemed where I belonged. It was my place.

Yet, at the age of 42, I had been considered a "misfit" by many of my fellow pastors—all because of one experience. I testified I had been baptized in the Holy Spirit and prayed in tongues.

Some people felt my tongues experience was an insidious "evil" which had suddenly taken hold of my life. The more traditional Baptist way of worship was "good" and proper—so, naturally, my new way of worshipping the Lord in an unknown tongue had to be "evil."

One retired Southern Baptist missionary canceled her

speaking engagement at our church when she learned I prayed in tongues. "People who pray in tongues are possessed by devils," she told me.

As the controversy slowly enveloped my respectable ministry of twenty years, I sensed my work as a Baptist pastor was coming to an end.

The gate slammed shut on me in a fleeting moment of reality one night during a telephone call. I had received many such calls from pulpit committees in recent days, but this call was from an old friend.

"Bill, this is Jerry Roper. How have you been? I haven't talked with you since you came back from Spain."

Jerry's voice was familiar to me. He and I had worked together as part of a ministerial team at a large Baptist church in Florida. That had been at the beginning of my ministry.

"It's good to hear from you, Jerry," I responded. "I understand you're coordinating the Baptist work in one of the fastest-growing areas of Florida. What brings you to call?"

"I've never been in such a challenging situation," he said excitedly. "People are moving into this area by the hundreds each week. Our growth is so fast we can't keep up with it."

"It sounds like you've got your hands full."

"That's true," he agreed. "One of our largest churches needs a senior pastor. The pastoral committee is looking to me for a recommendation. I've prayed about it and the Lord has told me you're the man for the job."

I was taken back by Jerry's brashness. Had he really heard from God? Did I actually have a ministry left in the Baptist church? I wondered if he had heard about my situation in Brunswick. Obviously not, or he wouldn't have called.

"I'd really like to work with you again," Jerry continued in rapid-fire. "We can raise up one of the greatest churches in the country right here. If you'll be in your pulpit Sunday morning, the committee will come hear you."

"Jerry, I'm honored," I said, searching for the words to tell my old friend what had happened in my life. "But you haven't seen me in a long time. You really need to know about some things that have happened in my life before you send a committee all the way to Brunswick."

"Oh, I know you, Bill Ligon," he laughed. "I've known you for years. You're like the Rock of Gibraltar. Your record is firmly established everywhere you've been. I'm not letting you off this easy, just so some other church can get you. I want you in my part of the state."

It was almost impossible to get Jerry to listen. He was absolutely convinced that he had chosen God's man for that Florida pastorate. Reluctantly, he agreed to listen.

"I've had a fresh experience with the Holy Spirit," I began softly.

"Great, Bill," he exuded. "That's what I want, a man who walks with God. That's essential to this work."

"But Jerry, you don't understand," I said. "When I had this experience with the Holy Spirit, I also began praying in tongues."

"What???"

The word stood up, end-on-end, as it rang through the telephone receiver. "You, too?" he shouted. "Bill, that's the devil's work!"

There it was again. Somebody else was judging my life in terms of their concepts of good and evil.

"But, Jerry, you were just saying a few minutes ago God had shown you I was the man for this job," I maintained calmly.

"I don't know what I said," he stammered, his voice cold and distant. "But you'll never fill any pulpit in my area if I can help it."

Before I could say another word, Jerry hung up. I was bewildered. A chill ran through my body. For the first time in my life, I felt as if I were being separated from something that was a part of me—like an arm or a leg.

I struggled with the temptation to give in to loneliness. More and more, lifelong friends dropped out of sight or were "no longer available" to talk with me. I had always been a team player in my denomination. I was always a member of the "in" group. But my experience with the Holy Spirit had shoved me into unfamiliar territory. I was no longer conforming to church tradition. That made me an "outsider"—and that was evil.

That kind of judgment was not hard to accept when some faceless pulpit committee suddenly lost interest because of my tongues experience, but a friend like Jerry Roper was different. Did this mean I didn't have a place in my denomination any more?

I felt I was the same person I had been before. But now some of my denominational brothers were calling my entire life "evil" because of one experience, an experience which I felt brought me closer to God.

Determined I wouldn't be forced out that easily, I told my wife I would be home in two days, and drove to Florida to talk with two retired Southern Baptist leaders who had known my work over the years. Surely they could advise me.

"I've told you everything that has happened," I explained to the first retired denominational leader. "For conscience's sake, I can't deny what God has done in my life. But the very experience that has increased my love for Jesus and my denomination is also creating a giant crisis in my church. Some of the same people who were instrumental in bringing me to Brunswick now consider me evil. I don't know whether to stay or leave. If I stay, I'm afraid the church will divide and I've never been one to divide people. I've always worked to unite them in the love of God."

Hearing about my baptism in the Holy Spirit didn't seem to shatter the respected Baptist leader. He wasn't quick to brand me an evil heretic as Jerry had. In fact, I felt the same interest and compassion he had when I was a younger pastor. I knew he had some answers.

"I saw the power of God move supernaturally to raise my wife off her deathbed," he said seriously. "I was on my face crying out to God to spare her life when the Holy Spirit let me know she had been healed. My faith was rewarded when I was told that same morning my wife would recover—so I don't doubt the power of God."

He stopped momentarily and sipped his coffee. My faith soared a little as he shared. "I have never prayed in tongues," he said. "I wouldn't oppose it if God gave me the gift, but—" and he paused.

I leaned forward to hear his words. "But, my brother, I do not believe there is a *place* for you now in Southern Baptist life. There are just too many influential people who will judge your experience as demonic. At best, they'll consider you emotionally unstable."

No place for me! The haunting words had come back

again. I felt as if I were being clipped from my very roots. I had found a home—a hiding place—in my denomination. Now all that was being taken away.

I drove on to see the other Baptist statesman. He startled me by explaining he had been baptized in the Holy Spirit with the gift of tongues since his retirement from the ministry. "At last," I thought, "somebody knows what I'm talking about."

At his suggestion, we attended a service later that night. During the evening an utterance in tongues came forth. I heard the interpretation as if the clouds had rolled back and God stepped forward saying, "This is what I want you to do."

"I have seen your work," came the interpretation. "I have been with you from the beginning of your work until now. I am closing doors which no man can open. I will open new doors which no man can close. Wait on me and see my work. Then you will see the day when those who oppose your work will be filled with the Holy Spirit."

I was overpowered by a paradoxical variety of emotions—joy and sadness, happiness and sorrow. The way of God was now clear but I could hardly believe what was happening. I knew I loved Jesus—yet I had known Him only in the context of the Baptist church. Now I was being separated from all that, and called to meet Him dressed in something other than a Baptist robe.

It all seemed so strange. That unsettled sense of being isolated, alone, remained in my subconscious. I knew it would be hard to find my place in the body of Christ. Yet deep inside I sensed God was calling me to a higher way than I had known—to lean directly on Him.

Five years passed. It was 1978. The prophecy of God continued to be fulfilled. God had opened new doors just as He said He would. I was in fellowship with people from all Christian denominations. The rapid growth of the body of Christ in Brunswick had eliminated any problems of being alone.

Pastors from other towns came looking for opportunities to fellowship. They too had wrestled with that sense of isolation or aloneness when church leaders turned away from them. That same problem apparently touched many lives. People all over the country appeared to be looking for places to establish security within the body of Christ.

Thousands of people who had been in denominational churches were being sovereignly baptized in the Holy Spirit. Like myself, they found themselves in need of two things. First, they needed someone to help them understand their new life in the Holy Spirit. Second, they needed a place where they could feel secure.

They wrestled with the problem of being isolated from their Christian tradition. Some felt alone. For years, they had associated Jesus with their denomination or specific church. Now that the Holy Spirit had broken down those barriers, they often found heated resistance to their new Holy Ghost experience. Many were considered undesirable—evil threats to their churches. Most felt rejected and without a place. Rejection left them with unresolved loneliness. Many reached out—even to extremist movements—seeking a place to belong.

It was this crucial truth that caused many to move into extremes of shepherdship or some form of community where rigid, absolute authority was exercised over their lives. Such authority made them feel secure. They had found someone who would assume responsibility for their lives. But instead of seeing this as a means to the greater end of individual responsibility, they settled down into it as an end in itself.

In the midst of their search, "new" teachings came from respected charismatic teachers saying every member of the body of Christ needed to find a shepherd and submit to him. The teachings suggested each "sheep" needed someone to assume responsibility for his life. The sheep, they said, could not see the ingrained flaws in his own character without the help of a sincere and qualified shepherd who would point out the sin and immaturity and set the example for a better way to live.

This unresolved conflict with the will of God prevented the disciple from enjoying blessings in the kingdom of God. He could not witness to others about Jesus because of his sin. Rigid discipline from a shepherd would identify that sin and remove it. The shepherd would enforce disciplines which would produce maturity in the disciple. Such maturity would please God and usher in added blessings. The disciple would be relieved from any isolation or loneliness as he developed a mature relationship with his shepherd.

"This is the answer," many lonely charismatics thought. "If I do that, I can find my place. My shepherd will show me my faults, guide me into maturity, and fill my need for fellowship."

Soon reports were criss-crossing the country from people who had gone into shepherdship. "The new relationship is just what I have been looking for to resolve my problems," many testified.

This very conclusion led numbers of people away from their brothers and sisters—causing upheaval of FGBMFI and Aglow chapters and the splintering of some charismatic fellowships and churches. Brothers separated themselves from others who were less committed. Many avenues for spreading the gospel were quickly disrupted.

Such was the case of a FGBMFI chapter in a Georgia town. Realizing the chapter was not satisfying some of their needs, a number of chapter leaders submitted themselves to a shepherd who had been active in the organization. At first, the men were told that submission to their shepherd would mature them in leadership. Next, a question was raised if there was "really" any need for the chapter to exist. Finally, the shepherd commanded his followers to withdraw from the chapter completely, leaving it without leadership. Weak and debilitated, the previously strong chapter floundered for months until new leadership could be raised up.

However, most of the people going into shepherdship never considered how they might get out from under heavy authority if their shepherd abused his office. That was the case of a former Southern Baptist pastor in Texas.

When he lost his church over the tongues experience, the veteran pastor felt rejection from fellow pastors and church leaders in his town. "I feel lonely," he told a nationally known shepherdship teacher at a conference.

"What you need is to find a shepherd and submit to him," the teacher advised. "You will not feel lonely again." That made sense to the pastor. He submitted to a shepherd who was submitted to the teacher.

Several years later, however, the pastor became uneasy about methods used to oversee his life. Complicated personal decisions related to his family were to be submitted to his shepherd for guidance. The shepherd, in turn, submitted the decisions to the national teacher when he did not have the "answer from God."

"The teacher has become the head of my household," the pastor observed one day. "My wife knows a difficult decision will be resolved by him. We have lost our place together with God. Instead of praying together to hear from God, the teacher hears for us. He is now our head."

When the pastor shared his observation with his shepherd, he was told he needed to deal with rebellion in his heart. His decision to break the relationship with his shepherd brought a stern rebuke.

"You will lose out with God on three counts if you break your relationship with me," he was told. "First, you will no longer be in the kingdom of God. Second, you will have no more authority with God. Third, you will never be financially successful."

As the pastor and his family broke the submitted relationship with their shepherd, they wrestled with fear and condemnation. In time, they were set free.

In another case, a charismatic pastor in Alabama wanted to demonstrate his love for brethren in shepherdship and his desire to walk in fellowship with them. As a result, he invited a national shepherdship teacher to his church to teach covenant and leadership principles of shepherdship. When the teaching series ended, five of the church's seven elders and half of the church membership broke with the pastor.

Surprised at the turn of events, the pastor inquired as

to why the departed members and elders had taken such action. "We are preparing to submit ourselves individually to shepherds in other towns," they answered. "We need someone to personally assume responsibility for our lives. We have not grown enough spiritually under your leadership. We look at the immaturity of our lives and realize someone must bring us into maturity. We have got to submit ourselves to their authority for it to happen."

It is a faulty supposition that a man will achieve spiritual maturity through a process of helping him identify the immaturity and sinful habits in his life. Such thinking has the tendency to ignore the role of the Holy Spirit in bringing a willing disciple into Christian maturity.

Teachers who work with the disciples of Jesus are only cooperating with the Holy Spirit. It is He who is the teacher and guide. Thus teachers and pastors must be careful not to usurp His place in the individual disciple's life.

By allowing a disciple to focus on his inadequacies and weaknesses, he will lose his place with God. He will not become wise or mature as it has been suggested. In time, the disciple will transfer his dependence from God to the shepherd who promised to make him wise.

God warned Adam and Eve of just such a danger: "Of every tree of the garden thou mayest freely eat: But of the tree of the knowledge of good and evil, thou shalt not eat of it: for in the day that thou eatest thereof thou shalt surely die" (Gen. 2:16-17).

Satan's intent was clearly to cause Adam and Eve to

lose their place with God. He achieved that by getting them to eat the forbidden fruit. But look what he told them: "Ye shall not surely die: For God doth know that in the day ye eat thereof, then your eyes shall be opened, and ye shall be as gods, knowing good and evil" (Gen. 3:4-5).

For once, Satan told the truth—if only a half-truth!

Man does have the capacity to explore good and evil—but such pursuit will not make him wise. It only uncovers a topsy-turvy world of fear and insecurity.

Throughout Church history, men have repeatedly failed to see this danger as they discipled others. Many discipleship efforts wandered into extremes and eventually failed because of such pursuit.

Jesus Christ is man's security. He is man's place. Disciples who learn these great truths have no need to explore the depths of good and evil. Their stability and maturity have already been established. They have found their place in Jesus. He is the solid rock upon which they have built.

3 | *The Need for Place*

As I sought for my own "place" in the Kingdom I was impressed with Dr. Paul Tournier's book, *A Place For You*. "In the beginning," Dr. Tournier wrote, "the Bible places man in the Garden of Eden. A place for him!"[1] Dr. Tournier noted that after Adam's sin and the murder of Abel by Cain, man became a wanderer on the face of the earth. Since that time, wandering man has attempted to find a place for himself. In the course of that search man has tried to localize God.

The problem is that God will not fit into any of man's preconceived molds. Man futilely tries to fence God into a particular locale. He even attempts to limit God's vast revelations to his own scope of thinking. If man can put God into a place, man thinks erroneously that he will have a place with God.

It is precisely such thinking that has caused fearful and insecure men to fall into lines of one-to-one submission across the country. Others have entered tightly-bound

[1] Paul Tournier, *A Place For You*, (New York and Evanston: Harper & Row, 1966), p. 39.

communities. All are looking for their place.

People know that God is speaking today. They know that God has spoken through certain anointed men. They are unsure God will speak directly to them. More than likely, they feel, He won't. Thus, they join up where they can get into the "life flow"—either in submission or community—of what God is supposed to be saying. Surely, if they get into that place, they will hear from God.

The "life flow" concept is supposed to be the panacea for the Christian life. Unfortunately, that is not the case.

Many persons have exchanged one false place of security for another. Such was the case recently of a man who had worked his way through the rigid requirements of his church to ordination as a priest. Not finding fulfillment there, he was drawn into the charismatic renewal.

Instead of discovering Jesus as his place, the former minister submitted himself to another man as his shepherd. Here, he expected to find the security he sought. Because of his solid theological background, he was invited to speak in a seminar in a nearby state—only to become embroiled in a personal conflict with the director.

When the retreat leader confronted the man about the problem, the former minister hid himself in the woods. Several hours later, the retreat director found the man alone—depressed and confused.

"I haven't worked under the authority of anyone but my shepherd," he lamented, "and I don't know what I'm supposed to do."

In effect, the man was saying, "I am out of my place. My

place is in relationship with my shepherd and I don't function properly if I'm not in that place. I'm only able to make decisions when I'm in my right place." He had never understood that a way was open so he could relate directly to God.

Jesus taught His disciples in Matthew 10:19-20 that when they were called before authorities, they would not even have to plan ahead on what they should say. Preparation had already been made. "It shall be given you in that hour what you are to speak," He instructed. "For it is not you who speak, but it is the Spirit of your Father who speaks in you" (NASB).

Jesus Christ as Place

As part of their training program (Matt. 10:5 NASB), Jesus briefed His disciples before sending them out into the world. "I send you out as sheep in the midst of wolves," He said (verse 16).

When the trials came, Jesus ironically gave them *no* instructions for trying to contact Him. That, too, was a vital part of the training program. The Spirit of God in them was to guide their speech. Jesus would be their place even in judgment halls before governors and kings. In that kind of atmosphere, the disciple was forced to rely upon God, or perish.

A disciple of Jesus Christ snould be able to function anywhere—alone in the courtroom, in jails as did Paul and Silas, in the local church, or in the quiet of the home. Wherever he is, the disciple is securely grounded in his place—the Lord Jesus Christ.

The apostle Paul had discovered this significant truth about the Christian life. He said, "I am convinced that neither death, nor life, nor angels, nor principalities, nor things present, nor things to come, nor powers, nor height, nor depth, nor any other created thing, shall be able to separate us from the love of God, which is in Christ Jesus our Lord" (Rom. 8:38-39 NASB).

Paul had found his place in God.

Hundreds of years before, David had proclaimed this same message. He said, "the eternal God is thy refuge" (Ps. 46:1). The word "refuge" can also be translated *dwelling place*. Somehow, David had reached the place in his spiritual maturity that he was able to rely upon God as his source in every situation.

When a certain scribe came to Jesus saying he wanted to be His disciple, Jesus answered, "the son of man has no *place* to lay his head" (Matt. 8:20). On the contrary, he said, the foxes have holes and the birds have nests. Jesus considered it important that His disciples understand they do not have a place in this natural world.

I believe Jesus wanted this man to see God as Lord and Master. He wanted the man to know that, as a disciple, the "eternal God becomes our *place*."

That understanding is essential to the disciple of Christ. Here again, Paul focused on a basic truth. He said he had reached the place of growth as a servant of Jesus that whatever circumstance (place) he was in, he was content (Phil. 4:11).

John 1:14 declares that the "Word became flesh." This Word or *logos* in Greek means the power that creates and sustains the life in the universe. This *logos* "dwelt among us"—*eskēnōsen en hēmin*—which means that God literally "pitched His tent" and "tabernacles" among men.

What then happened, man's place was forever

established in Christ. God had put a tabernacle on earth for man. He had given the place back to man which Adam had lost.

Place is undoubtedly the most important source of security in the natural man's life. A person in an older denominational church has his place. His membership has been established for years. The traditions of his church are formed.

His place as a person in the Christian community is clearly defined. He can tell you what street his church is located on and the time of the morning service. He may not be able to tell you what Jesus Christ means in his life, but he does have security. That security is most likely false but it will be hard convincing him of that. When his time comes to die, he may confess that he's not "sure" if he really knows Jesus.

While in seminary, I pastored a small Baptist church in a rural Kentucky community. One of the deacons faithfully chose the same place to sit each Sunday—a right front pew next to the wall. About halfway through each service, he religiously leaned his head back against the wall. In time, a grease spot formed.

For youth emphasis week, we named young people to temporarily hold all offices in the church. The deacon's nephew, a fifteen-year-old boy who was retarded due to a childhood accident, was chosen to take his uncle's place as a deacon. Without prompting from anyone, he sat in his uncle's pew and followed the older man's routine—leaning his head back in the greasy spot on the wall. His simple actions accented the importance of place in the average person's life.

Some might not think it unusual for place to be so

important in a denominational person's life, but I have seen the same need among supposed "free in the spirit" charismatics.

Our fellowship in Brunswick uses folding chairs for seating. If the chairs are ever set up in a direction other than normal, people have become disoriented when they walked into the room. At times, some have complained they actually "can't find their place." It seems people only feel secure when they have a familiar place to snuggle into.

Problems Caused by the "Search"

Problems in discipleship have developed because men have not understood this strong inner drive to find a place. Not realizing the consequences, many have bound themselves over to other people simply out of a need to be part of something or recognized by somebody. Unfortunately, many leaders do not seem to recognize this deep psychological need, and wrongly translate it into a need to "plug in."

Submission to the oversight of one person has been exhorted as "the way" to achieve maturity as a disciple. Actually the reverse is true. Commitment to Jesus Christ is the only road to mature character. Gene White's story best exemplifies this point.

Gene's sincere faith and love for the Lord had been recognized by a nearby fellowship as a pastoral calling. He had already demonstrated stability as a member of a classical pentecostal church. After prayer and consultation, the Brunswick fellowship installed him as pastor in the nearby town. It was his first pastorate.

In his inexperience and youth, some of the restless

members made Gene nervous. His wife also felt pressured by other women trying to mold her into a "proper" pastor's wife.

Since he had no formal pastoral training, Gene met with me weekly for prayer and counsel. "Take your time," I advised him. "Stay in the Word. Pray. Relate to your elders. They respect your office. But above all, be God's man." I had seen many young men come into maturity in this way. Our local fellowship continually prayed and I personally encouraged Gene.

His church was growing. Many were being added regularly but Gene seemed confused. I sensed he was torn between my advice and tapes on shepherdship he was frequently hearing. Frank Patterson had previously taught in that town. He encouraged Gene to submit himself to a shepherd as a way of establishing himself in the ministry. Frank even volunteered to "oversee" his work from Arkansas.

The struggle continued for several months. Then one day the dam broke. Gene came to me saying, "I've submitted myself to Frank in Arkansas. I believe this will secure me in the work."

Unfortunately, Gene's submission to Frank did not secure him at all. Within months, many of the people in the fellowship scattered. The once healthy group was dying a slow, painful death when Gene finally decided to move to Arkansas to be near Frank. The bewildered people left behind were even more confused. What happened?

In an effort to find his own place, Gene had lost sight of his mission as a shepherd to his people. The Bible says, "Where there is no vision, the people perish" (Prov.

29:18). When a shepherd or a body of believers loses sight of its mission, the dynamics is lost although the formality and mechanics may roll on religiously. Such is the case in many churches.

The Need for Support

Gene's tragic case has been repeated in many places in various parts of the country. Unable to see the nature of their relationship to Jesus, people have moved off into extremes to find fulfillment. Sincere men of God end up using principles taught in the New Testament for the development of Christian character as the basis for the organization of church government.

Why would men move away from balanced concepts of Christian fellowship into such rigid relationships with individual teachers?

I believe it is due to what Dr. Paul Tournier calls "the need for support." He says, "How great is the need of all men for support. It is a long time since it first struck me. That the weak, the lonely, the neurotic, people who have always lacked support, should seek it avidly is obvious and easy to understand. But the strong need it quite as much. It is less noticeable, because they hide it more easily."[2]

Dr. Tournier has uncovered the root of the problem. All men, weak or strong, need support. All seek support for each role they fill in life. When they find a place of security, they feel supported. When they discover a friend who accepts them "just as they are," they feel supported.

"All men are looking, in fact, for God's support," says Dr. Tournier. "Some are quite aware of the fact; in others

[2]Tournier, op. cit., p. 170.

it is only a vague nostalgic longing."

It seems as if all ages, races, creeds and colors are touched by this need for support. Little girls want to play "house." There is obvious security in that. Twelve-year-old boys have their "secret clubs" where no girls are allowed. College students have sororities and fraternities that meet this same basic need.

Even adults have secret societies or clubs where the select few are admitted. In most cases, they are WASP groups—white, Anglo-Saxon, Protestants. No Jews, blacks or Catholics are permitted. They take secret oaths and greet one another with a special handshake. The secrets they know and fraternal bonds they feel all bring about security. They have found a place.

Jesus called this support "a place for you" (John 14:2). He made it clear that God had provided unlimited resources for giving eternal support and salvation to men. God is the only one who can provide this eternal place (1 John 5:11-15).

If the church does not provide ways to secure this support, the ever-determined disciple will find it at great cost to himself. Many fellowships have been uprooted in the process. The drive to find his place will often blind the disciple to the Christ who provides it. Ignorant of what he is actually looking for, the disciple may even abandon the very principles Jesus taught to help him find it.

The struggle has repeated itself throughout Church history as disciples have searched for that "secret" which will unlock doors ushering them into greater heights of spiritual maturity.

4 | *Discipleship in Church History*

One solid impression emerges from studying Church history: Each new religious movement has been generated by a charismatic figure and an accompanying band of disciples.

When Jesus Christ broke into human history with His twelve disciples, it was not new to the nation of Israel to see such an arrangement. At the time of Christ's birth, the lands surrounding the Mediterranean Sea were in the possession of Rome. Hellenistic ideas—humanistic and classical ideals associated with ancient Greece —dominated the Roman Empire and greatly influenced the land of Israel.

In the Hellenistic culture, "discipling" was considered the only true way of teaching. It was a method used by renowned teachers such as Socrates, Plato and Aristotle who had small bands—much as Jesus did—who followed and sat at their feet.

Socrates (470-399 B.C.) taught by questioning his

hearers about their opinions and then asking further questions about their answers. His "gadfly" methods ultimately offended important people in Athens, and Socrates was found guilty of "introducing new gods and corrupting youth." His last days were spent in prison patiently instructing his disciples.

Plato (427-347 B.C.) was the best-known disciple of Socrates. Since the latter left no writings of his own, Plato wrote an account of his teachings. Plato taught in the same manner as Socrates, opening a school called the Academy because it was located in the Grove of Academus.

Aristotle (384-322 B.C.) studied under Plato for twenty years and was instrumental in the tutoring of the young Alexander the Great. When Aristotle lectured to his disciples, he used to walk along the corridors and shaded walks of the Lyceum at Athens.

Because of his early training, Alexander the Great admired Hellenistic ideas and he succeeded in spreading them throughout the nations he conquered. Thus Greek culture—which involved the logic of Plato—became a world culture and influenced the land of Jesus' birth.

Even before Jesus began His public ministry, the way was being prepared by John the Baptist, who stands as the last prophet in the Old Testament style who had his own disciples. John baptized his own disciples following the confession of sins and taught them a special prayer. When Jesus assumed His ministry, some of John's disciples saw Him as the promised Messiah and transferred their loyalty to Him. A few of John's followers continued independently and were found in Ephesus during Paul's ministry there (Acts 19). They, too, later followed Jesus rather than John. (Interestingly, Paul did not urge them to transfer allegiance to him as their shepherd, but to Jesus.)

During the first century, little bands of disciples apparently were drawing themselves around various preachers. Apollos was so popular at Corinth, a faction was gathering around him, while others were giving special attention to Peter or Paul. It is to this very question that Paul speaks in 1 Corinthians 1:11-13 and 1 Corinthians 3:4-6.

Problems over discipleship and church order have plagued the body of Christ since 44 A.D. Then, Jewish Christians in Jerusalem reluctantly gave in to recognizing the work of the Holy Spirit among the Gentiles at Antioch (Acts 11:1-2). The church heard from God on that issue (Acts 11:18) and clearly saw its evangelistic mission.

As a result, Antioch became the center for missionary outreach to the Gentile world, with the Jerusalem church supporting her efforts.

A Challenge to the Church

The Church has repeatedly lost sight of its mission throughout its long history. Each time that happened, strong men came forward insisting on reforms, and leaders gathered disciples around themselves. Their methods were not always the same. Some succeeded in calling the church to renewal. Others blindly rejected the structured church in its totality—teaching a different approach to the Christian life from the one Jesus seemed to proclaim.

When New Testament principles for church life were overlooked, the work usually died out. When believers had a clear understanding of the church's mission, the various renewal efforts found new disciples among the established church.

By 170 A.D. the organized church had lost confidence in complete reliance on the Holy Spirit for day-by-day guidance and polity, and turned to more rigid organization as a safeguard against heresies.

Lars P. Qualben in *A History of the Christian Church* says, "The church was no longer understood to be the holy people of God believing on Jesus Christ; but rather a group of persons belonging to the churches of the bishops."[1] A precedent had been set. The church was where the bishop was—not where the people were.

Communion with God was now understood to flow through a person's bishop or pastor. The life of the Spirit known by earlier generations of Christians was lost in the rigidity of organization. Into this setting walked Montanus of Arbada, the father of Montanism. Montanus found eager disciples among believers who were disenchanted with the formalism and relaxed discipline of the church. He offered a new, charismatic excitement as he called men to discipleship.

Kenneth Scott Latourette in *A History of Christianity* says that "Montanus spoke with tongues at his baptism"[2] and claimed that the Holy Spirit was giving him special revelations for the church. His emphasis on spiritual gifts and prophetic utterances attracted many followers, just as Pentecost did. It was easy for him then to impose a fanatical discipline on his followers.

There were numerous similarities between the behavior of the Montanists and the earlier New Testament church—such as manifestations of the miraculous gifts of the Holy Spirit, recognition of

[1]Lars P. Qualben, *A History of the Christian Church*, (New York: Thomas Nelson & Sons, 1942), p. 95.
[2]Kenneth Scott Latourette, *A History of Christianity*, (New York: Harper & Row, 1953), p. 128.

leadership roles through the Holy Spirit and belief in the soon return of the Lord Jesus Christ.

However, as Qualben notes in *A History of the Christian Church*, the Montanists "ushered in a new spiritual aristocracy."[3] They maintained that their teachings on the Holy Spirit were more advanced than that of the biblical tradition. The heresy broadened as they looked to their visions and revelations, which took on more importance than the written word of Scripture.

Tertullian (160-230), an ordained presbyter and father of Western theology, was Montanus' best-known disciple. His commitment added great influence to the movement. Montanism's ascetic and unworldly aspects appealed to Tertullian who broke with the "catholic" church in about 207. He died in continuing protest, apparently as the founder of a little sect of his own.

Montanism's influence extended down to the third and fourth century through the Novatianists and Donatists. It is not hard to see that Montanism had much truth mixed with some error. However, the eagerness of believers to experience renewal in their lives—the desire to find their "place"—made it difficult for them to detect error. It was a pattern to be oft repeated in continuing Church history—a pattern being repeated even today.

The Monastic Movement

By the third century, believers were back to seeking new ways to find their place in the body of Christ. Anthony of Egypt (250-346), the founder of Christian monasticism, commanded great attention when he emerged in 305 from an abandoned fort on the southern Nile where he had spent twenty years in prayer, fasting

[3]Qualben, op. cit., pp. 87-88.

and solitude. His self-imposed exile, his holiness and asceticism attracted hundreds of disciples, who adopted his rigorous way of life and took it with them into other places of Egypt, Palestine and Syria.

The goal of monastics was Christian perfection. Antionius (or St. Anthony) drew many disciples to his concepts. Qualben says that "hermits became so numerous in various localities that formations of hermit societies (cloisters) became necessary."[4] These monks believed they could attain Christian perfection if they abandoned the world and lived a disciplined, austere life.

The monastic movement became so popular and widespread among the young that by the fifth century the whole of the Catholic church was affected.

Latourette says that "at first it was primarily a lay movement, within the hierarchical structure of the clergy. To some degree it was a rebellion of the individual against the organization of the Catholic Church, regimented as it was under the bishops and clergy."[5]

Latourette also points out, in an effort to find spiritual security, the monk moved away from some basic principles taught by Jesus. His efforts to work out his personal discipline as a disciple caused him to abandon any missionary endeavor to win non-Christians.[6]

This tendency to draw away from the world into a cloistered community encouraged an "elite" attitude toward so-called "sub-Christians" who compromised with the world. The monk's selfish efforts to find his own place with God encouraged distant feelings toward other Christians. Yet his renunciation of all possessions and subsequent distribution of them to the poor gave him the feeling of unselfish devotion to others.

[4]Ibid., p. 109.
[5]Latourette, op. cit., pp. 221-222.
[6]Ibid., p. 222.

Founders of numerous monastic orders entertained dreams of forming Christian communities where the disciples would discover the secret of attaining Christian maturity. However, few of these men ever attained that satisfaction before their deaths, and those who did lacked the long-range vision to see that their approach to the Christian life was but "one of many" God had ordained.

Monasticism would probably have faded away early in its existence if it had continued looking inward to personal perfection and not outward in evangelism. Changes developed so that by the sixth century, many monastics—both men and women—became the devoted missionaries of the church's outreach. Additional modifications to monasticism made the orders supporters of the mission of the Catholic church instead of its enemy.

Benedictines—The First Catholic Order

The best known monastic order to develop during this time was founded by Benedict of Nursia (480-542). He first became a hermit at about fifteen or twenty years of age. Distressed by the widespread vices of his day, he diligently formed disciplines which soon brought him fame. Word spread that he had discovered the complete Christian life.

It was thought that Benedict had found his place in the kingdom of God. Latourette notes that parents brought their sons to him to be his disciples in hope of showing them how to find a better life.

"Benedict believed the best form of the life of a monk to be the cenobitic, that of the community," according to Latourette.[7]

His monasteries were to be self-supporting. Benedict

[7]Ibid., p. 334.

himself was recognized to have complete authority—remembering that in his authority he was accountable to God. Anyone wanting to come under this authority did so on a trial basis for one year. If the disciple then chose to stay, his decision was irrevocable and he surrendered all personal properties.

Pope Gregory the Great popularized the order and sent forth missionaries in foreign lands to establish themselves in similar monastic life.

As years passed, whenever the disciplines established by the founder declined, monastic life became easy and often scandalous. It was the relationship to one's superior and enforcement of rigid disciplines that kept the believer faithful. Although Benedict taught his disciples to "share the sufferings of Christ and deserve to be partakers of His Kingdom," the monk's commitment to Jesus was sometimes not as clearly defined as his commitment to the Order.

Subsequent declines in Christianity restored interest in monastic discipline and community life. Many—hungry to obtain salvation for their souls—sought after stronger, more devout leaders to follow. It was this inner need to find a place in God's kingdom which became the well-spring of monastic life.

Various revivals of monasticism adopted the disciplines of Benedict. At times, they made discipline even more austere and strict.

The monastery of Cluny, north of Lyons, is one in point. Its first abbot and founder was Berno. Many youths were attracted by his zeal and discipline. Again, parents sought to place their children in the Order for the attainment of wholeness of life.

By 1048, the Cluny monastery had extended its authority to sixty-nine other monasteries and scores of smaller groups called "cellae" (cells). By the twelfth century, their authority had broadened to more than three hundred monasteries.

It was the Cluny monastery which became the forerunner of such orders of friars as the Franciscans and Dominicans. Both orders, like many others, held noble missionary visions and submitted themselves unconditionally to papal rule.

After St. Francis of Assisi (1181-1226) obtained his papal approval from Innocent III in 1210 to establish his "Fratres Minores" or Lesser Brethren, his followers multiplied rapidly. Rigid personal disciplines were enacted. His followers practiced the utmost poverty, went about preaching repentance, singing much, aiding the peasants, and caring for the lepers and outcasts.

The Order grew so fast that by 1221 over 5,000 "brethren" attended a general chapter meeting. Their sole purpose was to live as "imitators of Christ" and thus obtain a better life. During that century the Order of St. Francis became one of the brightest lights in a church which was rapidly moving into darkness.

St. Dominic (1170-1221), a Spanish monk, was moved to establish the Order of Preachers, who under discipline and vows of poverty would preach to heretics. Papal approval came in 1216. This Order grew equally rapidly so that when Dominic died there were sixty houses in Spain, France, Italy, Germany and England.

Four obvious conclusions about man's pursuit of a place with God can be reached by an examination of monastic life in Church history. First, believers thought they could achieve a perfect life by submitting themselves to rigid discipline and withdrawing from corrupt worldly life.

Second, whenever laxity occurred in a religious order, new movements surfaced demanding that rigid discipline be restored.

Third, movements to restore loyalty to the Christian faith were only as strong as their leaders. When the leaders passed off the scene, the orders usually lost their strength.

Fourth, the ability to attain Christian maturity was centered in a person's submission to the discipline of the community. Such emphasis on discipline as the way to maturity often overshadowed divine grace.

Loyola, Luther and Calvin

Several strong leaders emerged in the fourteenth century stating that discipline in the Christian community was not enough to achieve Christian maturity. John Wycliffe (1320-1384) and John Huss (1369-1415) were among those calling for reform. Both proclaimed that justification before God was by faith in Jesus Christ only—that fulfilling men's rules did not substitute for personal repentance and individual faith.

Girolamo Savonarola (1452-1498) called on all citizens of Florence in 1486 to "accept Christ as their King." Such public declarations that submission to the authorities would not gain man a place with God later influenced officials to put both Huss and Savonarola to death.

Wycliffe's followers, who were first called "poor priests" and later Lollards, were suppressed by force. Their only crime appears that they openly petitioned Parliament for a reform of the church and attempted to spread the message of the Bible. They were the early forerunners of the English reformation.

The year 1540 is significant because it marked the beginning of greater opposition for Martin Luther (1483-1546) due to the bigamous marriage of Philip of Hesse. John Calvin (1509-1564) was called back to Geneva to begin his famous work and Ignatius Loyola (1491-1556) received approval from the Pope to begin the Society of Jesus.

Yet, as each of these men—reformers and Roman Catholic alike—felt the power of authority, they committed reprehensible acts against their opponents. Such atrocities represented a definite lack of balance in their work.

Luther, Calvin and Loyola all rose to unique positions of authority and prominence as a result of earnest quests to discover the place of Jesus Christ in their individual lives. Loyola, a Spanish ex-military man, who later founded the Society of Jesus (Jesuits), presents a classic picture. He began in a humble search for his place with Christ and ended up as the leader of an assembly of well-trained, militant disciples.

While recovering from injuries sustained in battle, Loyola read books on the life of Christ, St. Dominic and St. Francis. Moved by the dedication of these men, he gave his life as a spiritual knight to the service of the Holy Virgin.

Once recovered, Loyola went to a Dominican monastery in Manresa, Spain, where he passed through a great spiritual crisis. Alone in a cave, he prayed and fasted. After experiencing release through total self-surrender, he, like Luther, fell into difficult struggles with the devil. At Manresa, he worked out his "Spiritual Exercises" which he later used as a part of the rigid discipline of his disciples.

His disciples saw themselves as an army of soldiers ready to fight under the direction of the Pope. Latourette says to achieve this aim "they took a special vow to do whatever the Pope commanded 'for the good of souls and the propagation of the faith' in whatever countries he might wish to send them."[8]

Qualben says Loyola "found peace in complete subjection to the authority of the Church and its Tradition. . . . Loyola's religion demanded the crucifixion of the individual conscience in complete obedience to the authority of the Church."[9]

Loyola's energetic militancy attracted thousands of disciples. Although they saw themselves as the extension of God's kingdom on earth—a truth which all Christians should grasp and believe—they also saw themselves as the guardians against all heretical teachings which conflicted with the doctrines of the church at Rome.

Conscious of the "heresies" of the reformers, Loyola gathered his disciples and sent them out—not only to perform "good works" but also to punish heretics. In spite of the Order's great benevolent works, the fact cannot be overlooked that many believers outside the Roman church lost their lives in the Spanish Inquisition which Loyola strongly supported. It was not until much later that the vision of the Jesuits was lifted to more nobler causes.

Luther, who stated he had become a Doctor of Theology before he came to know the light that is Jesus Christ, was equally zealous. Qualben wrote that "Luther had for

[8]Ibid., p. 847.
[9]Qualben, op. cit., p. 340.

many years tried to take the Kingdom of Heaven 'by force.' Like Jacob of old, he had 'striven with God.' "[10]

It was only when Luther grasped the truth of Romans 1:17—"Man is justified by faith alone and not by works"—that he determined to reevaluate his "place" with God. His efforts to reform the church won him many followers. He, too, gathered disciples through his preaching, teaching and writing.

Qualben says that Luther saw the need to teach "each person to read and study the Bible." The common people were to "participate intelligently in the church services, and take an intelligent part in the affairs of state."[11]

The rapid response of peasants to Luther's teachings as well as pressure from the church of Rome made it necessary for Luther to move progressively to responsible authority over his new disciples. He arranged "an evangelical order of Divine Service" and organized "evangelical churches," according to Qualben.[12]

Qualben observed, "Luther's idea of the separation of church and state were entirely too advanced for the time. The people were not capable of governing their own church affairs and Luther's faith in the 'common man' was somewhat shaken after the Peasant War."[13]

The peasants seized their new freedom quickly. Williston Walker noted that "in March 1525, the peasants put forth twelve articles, demanding the right of each community to choose and depose its pastor, that the great tithes (on grain) be used for the support of pastor and other community expenses. . . ."[14] They also demanded other reforms in work laws and social life.

Qualben estimated a hundred to a hundred fifty thousand people lost their lives in the Peasants' War

[10]Ibid., p. 229. [11]Ibid., p. 241. [12]Ibid., p. 241. [13]Ibid., p. 243.
[14]Williston Walker, *A History of the Christian Church*, (New York: Charles Scribner's Sons, 1945), p. 354.

which followed.[15] The war had been fanned by Luther's demand that the princes crush the peasant revolt "with the sword."[16]

Such strong reaction on Luther's part caused him to lose the respect of many peasants. At the same time, Luther turned to the upper classes to exercise authority over the church. He placed the church under their supervision. His efforts to bring the masses together in churches without authority created confusion. Unprepared to establish balanced authority, he was pushed into abusive extreme.

Calvin—like Luther and Huldreich Zwingli—stated the Bible was the sole rule for faith and life. He saw the literal establishment of the kingdom of God on earth through government. Christ was to govern an entire city through the college of pastors and a theocracy based on Old Testament Israel.

In carrying out his plan, Calvin selected a group of morally upright men and made them responsible for the moral conduct of citizens of Geneva, Switzerland. These men, often called presbyters or pastors, controlled the social and cultural lives of individual persons down to the smallest detail. He instituted severe discipline on all—turning Geneva into a massive Christian community in the process.

Calvin's punishments became so severe that Michael Servetus, a famous Spanish physician, was burned at the stake in Geneva because of his anti-Trinitarian views. Calvin's efforts to govern church and state through rigid forms of mass discipleship blinded him to the words Jesus gave the Pharisees: "I will have mercy and not sacrifice" (Matt. 9:13).

[15]Qualben, op. cit., p. 244.
[16]Walker, op. cit., p. 354.

A pattern was emerging. Discipleship under men calling for unilateral submission to their rule invariably became authoritarian. Freedom was taken away. Virtual dictatorships were formed. Persecution of believers often followed. Calvin's dream for Geneva as a Christian community lasted less than a generation, although his followers tried in vain to establish his principles in many European cities extending even to the monarchy of England. All eventually collapsed.

English Reformers

The reformation efforts of Luther and Calvin were only the beginning of reforms within the church. England was a microcosm of what was happening elsewhere. Reformers there began movements which were bigger than any single man.

Qualben says, "William of Occam (1280-1349), the most influential theologian of his time, was one of the early forerunners of the English Reformation. He asserted that the pope was not infallible, that the General Council and not the pope was the highest authority in the church, that Holy Scripture was the only infallible source in matters of faith and life, and that in secular matters the church and the pope were subordinated to the state. Occam exerted a strong influence upon John Wycliffe and Martin Luther."[17]

Not realizing the strength of reform teachings in his own land, Henry VIII formed his own national church by cutting the English church from Rome. Though ties with Rome had been severed for political and personal reasons, the doctrines of apostolic succession, the historic episcopate and sacramental liturgics were retained in the

[17]Qualben, op. cit., p. 318.

Anglican church. All Henry wanted was a reformed Catholic church, national in all respects but under his control.

Disappointed, many leaders who were influenced by reform doctrines demanded that reforms in the newly formed English state church be continued until the church was purged. They demanded a *purer* form of worship, the establishment of a presbyterian form of church government, and the revision of church doctrine to agree with Calvinism.

The Puritans established an academic center at the University of Cambridge for the training of new pastors in the Calvinistic doctrines. They moved into every area of economic life in the country, gaining wealth and influence as they went. Disciples of Puritanism increased rapidly—making their voices heard throughout England.

"Thomas Cartwright (died the same year as Elizabeth), strongly influenced by the Genevan Calvinists, spoke from his position as professor of divinity at Cambridge University in favor of a thoroughgoing reform along Presbyterian lines."[18]

Cartwright and Walter Travers jointly authored the "Book of Discipline" setting forth the Puritan platform. Cartwright lost his professorship because of his call for reforms. His actions polarized reformers along lines of church government. The Puritans moved toward government by presbytery while Independents put it in the congregation's hands.

Disciples of Puritanism formed small Bible study groups. They gave strict adherance to Sunday observance and held special meetings for worship. They demanded that each adult testify to an experience of saving grace

[18]Frederick A. Norwood, *The Development of Modern Christianity Since 1500*, (New York: Abingdon Press, 1956), p. 100.

with Jesus Christ. In small group meetings, teachers taught the importance of self-discipline, individual Bible study and family worship in the home. A wealth of new Christian literature came into print. Except for absence of charismatic gifts in worship, it had all the appearance of a twentieth-century charismatic renewal.

While holding membership in the Church of England and demanding reforms they had defined, the Puritans submitted to authority in their Bible study groups which functioned under extra-social presbyteries. The seeds of sectarianism were planted. The birth of numerous denominations would follow.

Presbyterianism, which had been structured within the membership of the Anglican church, separated to follow reformers like John Knox of Scotland. Even today, the Westminster Confession of Faith spells out the authority of the Presbyterian church for belief and church order.

Meanwhile, the Independents had severed all connections with the established church. Disciples gathered around Robert Browne, but his leadership was continually disrupted with imprisonment and exile for his views. He organized the first congregation of English Independents at Norwich in 1580—causing the early Independent movement to be called "Brownists."

In 1582 he published a book called *A Treatise of Reformation without Tarrying for Anie, and of the Wickednesse of those preachers which will not reforme . . . till the Magistrate commaunde and compel them.* The book established a concept of independent, local congregations which later influenced the congregational governments of the Baptist and Congregational churches.

Separatist believers formed two new congregations,

one at Gainsborough under John Smyth and the other at Scrooby under John Robinson and William Brewster. Fleeing persecution, Smyth led his group to Amsterdam in 1607 where it came under the influence of the Mennonites, one of the true martyr churches in Europe.

Through the wisdom of the Mennonite founder, Menno Simons, the English Baptists were steered away from the radical teachings of the Munsterites, a militant Anabaptist group which "lived by the sword."

Simons, a former Roman Catholic priest, laid a foundation which insisted on a spiritual rebirth for each member. Mennonite disciples were taught to be separated from the evil world. They dressed simply, opposed liturgical forms of worship, and practiced foot-washing and the Lord's Supper. They also stressed character development based on Christ's Sermon on the Mount instructions.

Smyth led his group back to England, forming the first Baptist church there in 1612. Some of their followers accompanied the Pilgrims to America in 1620, founding Baptist churches in the new land. Disciples of Robinson from the Scrooby group also came to America, forming Congregational churches.

In 1646 George Fox, the son of a Presbyterian weaver, testified of an experience where an "inner light" spoke to him in the very voice of God. A small band of disciples quickly gathered around Fox as he traveled throughout England testifying of his experience. Thrown into prison for sharing his experience, Fox preached to the inmates and the jailers. They, too, experienced the inner light, often accompanied by physical manifestations of body movements. The Quakers had been born.

Fox's disciples rejected all outward forms of organized Christianity such as sacraments, ritual, creeds, preaching from pulpits, and professionally training men for the ministry.

Quaker worship services were filled with testifying and prophesying. Fox's followers often waited in silence to hear the "inner voice" which put words of wisdom and truth in the believer's mouth. Any believer who received such a "word" could share it in the meeting—giving rise to lay preaching.

Disciples of Fox grew so rapidly he had to organize. He named elders as leaders over each "flock" and established discipline for the church. Discipline subordinated the Bible to the "inner light," made all sacraments symbolic, declared every member a priest unto God, gave women the right to preach and teach as well as men, and declared all liturgy and formal worship idolatry—including all music and singing.

A pattern was established. As the church slipped from the original moorings of a group of believers called out of the world who adhered to faith in Christ as the top priority of life, charismatic leaders emerged who sought, through various means of discipleship, to call the church back to basics.

However, the people, all of whom had been deprived of the understanding of their right to an individual "place" in God, rallied around their leaders—declaring they wanted to "plug in" to human expressions of God. The leaders, most of whom were psychologically scarred by their own battles, gradually allowed movements to form around them or their doctrinal emphasis. When they were gone, men of lesser vision defined these movements into "orders" or "denominations," i.e., Franciscans, Dominicans, Lutherans, Mennonites, Presbyterians, Baptists, Episcopalians.

Piety, The Moravians and John Wesley

By the middle of the eighteenth century, the Age of Reason had already plunged the church in England and Europe into spiritual darkness. Intellectuals had convinced many that the "force" which stood behind true "enlightenment" was human reason. Men such as Voltaire, Rousseau, Gibbon, Kant, Bayle and Adam Smith influenced men to reject the miraculous as superstition.

Norwood notes, "Deists would consider theology a branch of physics."[19] They taught an impersonal Supreme Being who was to be worshiped. The "enlightenment" of men unfortunately left no place for the sovereign acts of God in the redemption of man.

Deism infiltrated the churches throughout England and Europe. Members were told from the pulpits of their churches that "the way to receive enlightment was by exercising the reason of the mind."

Philip Spener and August Francke, two educated pastors in Germany, skillfully brought direction back into the church. They asserted that right life was more important than right belief and experience with Jesus Christ was more important than intellectual assent. Thus they emphasized repentance, conversion and sanctification. In the process, they became the fathers of Pietism, the devout believer's reaction against deism.

The Moravian church embraced many of the doctrines taught by the Pietists. Influenced by the earlier life and

[19]Ibid., p. 118.

work of John Huss, the Moravians were in search of leadership and asylum after his execution. They finally settled on the estate of Count Nicholas Ludwig Von Zinzendorf in Saxony, becoming his disciples.

"Characterized by a semimonastic life including the separation of children from their parents for training and education, the little group grew, spread through missionary activity, and exerted an influence far beyond the pressure of numbers."[20]

A rigid discipline was set up by church officials. Unmarried persons were divided by sex, with no social life permitted between them. Believers were organized into "classes" for instruction in the Christian life. Smaller groups called "bands" were also formed. Members in "bands" were expected to open their conscience to the other members in a confession of all their sins.

Since Zinzendorf never expected to break with the Lutheran church, he expected his "classes" to work within Lutheranism. He believed that close oversight of the "believers" with confession of any sin would develop a holy and devout life.

The Moravians were an energetic and missionary-minded people. Their great vision of world missions took them to other continents. On one such journey, they introduced the Anglican priest John Wesley (1703-1791) to Jesus Christ, although Wesley's personal experience came later. In spite of their rigid community life, the Moravians succeeded in holding to Jesus Christ as man's source of eternal security.

Wesley appropriated the concept of "classes" and "bands" from the Moravians. He used them to organize the large numbers of Anglicans who came to him seeking a

[20]Ibid., p. 121.

mature relationship with Christ.

He called his classes "societies" and required that his disciples be assigned to them by sex and marital status. To "beef up" the lax morals of some members, he formed the smaller "band" groups. Anyone who joined a "band" had to be prepared to share his most intimate secrets and receive mutual rebuke for the same.

It was the eloquent preacher George Whitefield (1714-1770) who influenced Wesley to avoid the dangers of limiting the Christian community to only small groups. Many were being brought to Christ through Whitefield's mass meetings.

Thus Whitefield's open-air preaching gave Wesley a good example of outreach evangelism. It became an important tool to encourage future growth in Methodism. Without it, the small bands could have evolved into closed, self-centered "bless me clubs."

A crowd of 3,000 came the first time Wesley preached in the open air. Wesley saw the need for balance. He determined to both evangelize the lost and disciple believers in small groups.

"Societies" flourished under Wesley's preaching as new converts applied for membership. Latourette states that "he himself kept an autocratic control of the whole."[21] He frequently used dictatorial powers to keep everything in line until his death.

Perhaps the saving factor—that kept Wesley's work flourishing after his death—was the fact he had moved the "societies" into their own buildings where local churches could be formed. An air of permanency developed in his work. Although Wesley proclaimed his loyalty to the Church of England until his death, his disciples began the

[21]Latourette, op. cit., p. 1027.

Methodist church against what Wesley described as "my own wishes."

English Methodism Declines

The teaching of Wesley and Whitefield had been a bold answer to German rationalism, French atheism and English deism which swept Europe and England. Latourette states, "Most of the early Deists were English. This may have been in part because of the multiplicity of the forms of Christianity in England. . . . In the eighteenth century, especially after 1750, Deism was to have a wide vogue not only in the British Isles, but also on the Continent."[22]

Concern for the outcast diminished in the Methodist movement following Wesley's death. C.P.S. Clarke notes, "Methodism settled into respectability."[23] His disciples closed themselves off in their church buildings in an attempt to strengthen one another through fellowship.

Wesley's message of hope was returned in 1866 to the poor and common people by a Methodist pastor, William Booth (1829-1912). He first called his organization the "Christian Mission" but later changed it to "The Salvation Army."

Disciples quickly gathered around Booth. In 1878 he introduced military features into his organization. Clarke points out that his plans resembled the absolute authority Ignatius Loyola had incorporated into the Jesuit Society when Roman Catholic devotees submitted themselves to him.[24]

Booth retained Methodist doctrine but adopted Charles G. Finney's methods of mass evangelism. His plans for international outreach were taken from the

[22]Latourette, ibid, p. 984.
[23]C.P.S. Clarke, *Short History of the Christian Church*, (Longmans Green and Co. Ltd., London, 1963), p. 416.
[24]Clarke, op. cit., p. 416.

missionary-minded Moravians. Although other churches at the time did not do so, women were given prominent positions in the Army's official work. Officers had rank as in the military and operated under orders of their superiors. Disciples in local congregations were submitted to the local commander. Extra-local discipleship on a governmental basis only was practiced by the commanders.

The Salvation Army continues today due primarily to the establishment of local congregations, which give fellowship to Army "soldiers" and the strong, disciplined organization Booth emplanted before his death.

Booth's Salvation Army was one of three directions Methodists took who chose not to remain in the more formal Methodist churches. The first direction, of course, was a continuation of the mainline Methodist church. The third direction had pentecostal overtones. Disturbed by the French Revolution and the Napoleonic wars, which they believed were ushering in the Last Judgment, disenchanted Methodists gathered in homes throughout Scotland and England. They prayed for restoration of the "true work of the Holy Spirit in the Church." Their meetings had pentecostal overtones, including speaking in tongues.

Ironically, the leader and founder of the new movement was Edward Irving (1792-1834), a Presbyterian minister from Scotland. Qualben says the groups were organized into the "Catholic Apostolic Church" in 1835. According to Qualben, Irving "looked upon the entire development of the Church since the days of the Apostles as a great apostasy.

"He proclaimed that the Last Judgment was near and

that all 'true Christians' were to be blessed with the supernatural gifts and endowments of the Apostolic church before the coming of the Lord. In 1836 the Irvingites organized all of Christendom into twelve tribes with an apostle for each tribe. After 1867 all true Christians were 'sealed,' on the basis of Rev. 3:7f, by the laying of hands. The second coming of Christ was to occur as soon as 12,000 had been sealed in each tribe."[25]

Irving, giving emphasis to Paul's teaching in Ephesians 4, established a strong organization of apostles, prophets, evangelists and pastors for the oversight of the church. His liturgy was based on the Eastern rites. All twelve apostles were to be in place when the Last Judgment began.

Despite the fact Irving misjudged end-time doctrine, he seemed to understand the balance needed between charismatic power and apostolic authority in the church. However, he failed to understand New Testament concepts of apostolic ministry and placed too much authority in his apostles. As the apostles died off, the church of his dreams decayed. His people, who relied totally upon their apostle set over them, were unable to follow the authority of Christ. With no continuing authority, the church fell into decline.

By this time the churches born in the fire of reformation had settled into organizational security. Differences in church government had produced numerous denominations. The many "Protestant churches"— devoid of the Holy Spirit's power through charismatic gifts—had made a complete cycle. They had returned to the coldness and indifference their forefathers had protested. Much of this new Christian posture had

[25]Qualben, op. cit., p. 407.

already been transported to the new world of America, setting the stage for the rise of a new pentecostalism at the beginning of the twentieth century.

5 | *Discipleship in the Western Hemisphere*

Spiritual decay within society has always driven devout men to their "prayer closets" seeking God. The Almighty responded through anointed preachers—much like John the Baptist—calling the masses to repentance.

The new disciples clustered together in common bonds of fellowship asking, "Where do we go from here?" Their leaders answered by organizing communities and churches, and teaching the "Christian life" as they understood it. Success laid the foundation for another denomination. Second generation leadership carried on the work—using methods of the founders, but generally oblivious of the Holy Spirit who had birthed the "new" movement in the first place.

This well-established trend found its way countless times into Church history before and during the twentieth century. Each time, God sovereignly moved again to call men out of their lifeless religion into a personal relationship with himself. Each time, the bands of disciples slipped into the bondage of tradition. Invariably the power of the Holy Spirit was quenched.

The Great Awakening in America
(1734-1744)

Mass evangelism has always been the tool of God to set the stage for the discipling of His people. Those who responded to the call were enlisted in training programs. Some methods produced stable, mature believers while others failed miserably.

Such was the case in both England and the New World. While Wesley and Whitefield were calling people out of spiritual darkness caused by German rationalists, French atheists and English deists, renewal was taking place in the American colonies.

By the first half of the eighteenth century, church life in the American colonies had declined spiritually. Worship was cold and formal. Clergymen were lazy, immoral and bigoted. Churches were filled with unregenerated people. Under the dominating shepherdship of Cotton Mather, actions were taken to stop the occult practices of witches. At the same time, Baptists and Quakers were being fined, flogged and imprisoned for resisting the authority of the Church of England.

As always, God's answer to the problem was another anointed prophet calling for repentance. It began with Jonathan Edwards (1703-1758), a well-educated Congregationalist pastor, who came under the burden to call his decadent country back to God. Edwards preached thunderous doctrinal sermons throughout New England.

His famous sermon, "Sinners in the Hands of an Angry

God," caused great fear of judgment to come upon people. One-seventh of New England's population was converted. Churches were filled with new believers excited about their relationship with God. They were eager to be taught the ways of God.

Yet by the close of the eighteenth century, the strong Congregational churches which came from the Great Awakening had failed to extend their influence much outside of New England. Instead of maintaining an evangelistic spirit like Edwards, they focused inward—trying to interpret church government.

Strong emphasis on the autonomy of the local congregation decentralized their work completely. Each congregation was left to interpret the whole of the Christian movement relatively alone. Congregations debated the theology of Jonathan Edwards and the value of revivals. Unitarian doctrine—publicly renouncing belief in the deity of Christ—crept in, bringing further division to the churches. The value of the individual convert was lost in the singular emphasis on the congregational life of the church.

Despite the fact that many Christian communities were formed, some even giving birth to colleges and universities to train disciples, without the power of the Holy Spirit all degenerated into human efforts.

Circuit-Riding Preachers

John Wesley expected Methodism to be a movement within the Church of England, and nothing more. His concern was to disciple believers into mature Christian character. But his plan of appointing itinerant lay preachers to minister to his "societies" laid the foundation for a new denomination.

When the bishops of the Church of England refused to ordain Methodist preachers for the work in America, Wesley did it himself, naming Dr. Thomas Coke as "superintendent." He ordained Richard Whatcoat and Thomas Vasey as presbyters (or elders). They were instructed to ordain Francis Asbury as joint superintendent of North America.

Asbury refused appointment by Wesley, choosing to be elected by unanimous vote of the Methodist Conference. In 1787 he changed his title to "bishop" resulting in a severe reprimand from Wesley. He kept the title, though, with the approval of the majority of the preachers, who overrode Wesley's desire.

Asbury's plan of using preachers mounted on horseback to search out people and bring them to God revolutionized the new settlements springing up. His young, brave riders preached and sang to thousands just as the Franciscans had done. Their greatest love was to see a person confess faith in Jesus Christ.

Dramatic things occurred when the circuit riders preached sanctification as a "second work of grace." People from all confessions of faith fell to the ground as if dead. Some experienced visions and heard God speak while transfixed as in a trance. Others laughed and danced.

The circuit riders gathered their new converts into classes of twelve or more to disciple them, naming a class leader for supervision. Several classes made up a "society" or a local group of Methodists. Several societies formed a "circuit" with one preacher assigned to oversee them. Several circuits formed a district under a presiding elder. Above the elders were the bishops or superintendents with absolute control over the denomination. Qualben points out that not until William McKendree was elected bishop in 1808 was the one-man autocracy of Asbury changed to a constitutional and "settled legal order."[1]

Formality and Institutionalism

Methodist, Baptist and some other groups began to use theological institutions to train their leadership by the middle of the nineteenth century. Highly trained professors taught the future church leaders that manifestations or gifts of the Holy Spirit were out of place in Christian worship. The value of small group relationships was lost as churches grew numerically and institutions were established to train disciples.

As the frontier changed and people evolved in education and wealth, they settled down to a more formal manner of worship. "A churchman should avoid emotionalism and learn to control himself," it was suggested. Understanding the work of the Holy Spirit was lost as men overreacted to extremes within the church. Education of church leadership was left in the hands of professionally trained men. Local membership was trained in Bible classes. Once again, the church returned to institutionalism.

Teachings on Holiness Break Out

About 1880, people within the Methodist church complained the church had become too formal. Many believed that Wesley taught a doctrine of "entire sanctification" where the carnal nature of man was

[1]Lars S. Qualben, *A History of the Christian Church* (New York: Thomas Nelson & Sons, 1942), p. 543.

destroyed. This gave man a "holy" standing with God.

Some said the more formal members of the church were not coming into holiness. There was no place for "heart religion" like that of the old days. Many remembered how Wesley's doctrine of "perfect love" or "sanctification" brought the power of the Holy Spirit into their lives. People wanted a return to these times.

Other Methodists had settled into tradition. They wanted a more formal, dignified manner of worship and refused to compromise. The rift resulted in the formation of small groups within congregations. They met to study teachings on justification, cleansing and the "second blessing."

The crisis peaked in 1890. Numerous groups seeking the "holy life" broke with the Methodist church and formed various holiness denominations. The largest, and still growing today, was the Church of the Nazarene, formed in 1894.

Before and after this period there were also other interdenominational holiness movements, spearheaded by such noted evangelists as Charles W. Finney, Dwight L. Moody and R.A. Torrey. Moody Bible Institute in Chicago was founded to perpetuate this movement.

However, the largest number of new members and leaders came from the Methodist church. The new groups disagreed slightly on doctrines of sanctification. Some church members received the gift of tongues while others refused to include teaching on this gift.

The holiness movement became the forerunner of the modern classical pentecostal movement. The charismatic gift of tongues—manifested first at Pentecost (Acts 2:4)—became the main issue in the formation of pentecostal churches. It separated the proponents from their holiness brothers who denied the gift was valid for their day.

Pentecostal Fires

By the dawn of the twentieth century, Protestant Christianity had never reached such heights of scholarship. Roman Catholics were established throughout the world. Jews had gathered in great numbers in the United States. Since Bethlehem, God had not chosen more humble surroundings to demonstrate His love to man. Before it was over, every major religious body—Catholic, Protestant, Jewish—would be touched by the pentecostal fires.

It all started in 1900 when a young Methodist minister, Charles F. Parham, decided he would open a Bible school where he would be both director and student. He found a building in Topeka, Kansas, still a pioneer area of the nation, and announced that anyone who wanted to join him there to study the New Testament was welcome. Forty students showed up with their wives and children.

Parham, who had been influenced by reports from the Welsh pentecostal renewal, led his students into a study of the book of Acts. The group of learners decided that the baptism in the Holy Spirit with the manifestation of tongues was a valid experience. They prayed from morning until evening on New Year's Eve, 1900, without success.

At seven o'clock that night, one of the students, Agnes N. Ozman, asked Parham to lay hands on her to impart the gift of the Holy Spirit. When he did, Agnes began to speak in a language neither understood.

Five years later, after experiencing many successes and reverses in his new charismatic ministry, Parham opened a second Bible school in Houston, Texas. William J. Seymour, an ordained black minister, enrolled as a student. He soon was baptized in the Holy Spirit with the gift of tongues.

In 1906 Seymour arrived in Los Angeles to preach in a black Church of the Nazarene. The church leaders were not prepared for him to open his revival with a sermon on the baptism in the Holy Spirit with the gift of tongues. The next night, they locked Seymour out of the church.

A woman in the Nazarene Church opened her home to those who wanted to hear Seymour's message. For several nights, he preached on the New Testament experience with the Holy Spirit. Then, on the evening of April 9, 1906, as Seymour was speaking, people began to speak in tongues, laugh and shout.

Revival broke out and a larger building was needed. Ironically, an abandoned Methodist church, which had been converted into a stable, was located. Blacks and whites crowded into the building night after night. The response shook the state. Word spread rapidly across country that God was visiting people in a building at 312 Azusa Street, Los Angeles. People came all the way from the East coast to experience the pentecostal power. The revival lasted all day, all night, for over 1,000 days.

Pentecostal Denominations Surface
New Spirit-filled pilgrims returned to their homes throughout the world, bearing good news of their fresh experience with the Holy Spirit. Many new churches were formed, as people in small gatherings were baptized

in the Holy Spirit. Holiness churches were led into the classical pentecostal movement or were split over the teaching on tongues.

The holiness crisis of the mid-1890s had already introduced division into Methodism. Hundreds of Methodist preachers left in protest to new trends they saw in the church. Recognizing that church members were spiritually dead and not knowing what to do about it, they demanded holiness as evidence the believers were mature. They formed holiness churches adopting the same methods which had led earlier groups back into spiritual decay.

The influence of the Azusa Street revival gave fresh hope to young holiness denominations. Among them were the Church of God, Cleveland, Tennessee, formed in 1886; the Pentecostal Churches of America, formed in 1894; and the Church of God in Christ, in 1895. The Pentecostal Holiness Church was established in 1898, only to merge with the Fire-Baptized Holiness Church, which had been organized three years earlier. The 1911 merger brought about the present-day Pentecostal Holiness Church.

G.B. Cashwell of Dunn, North Carolina, was one of the first Pentecostal Holiness ministers to be baptized in the Holy Spirit. Cashwell had been a Methodist pastor before joining the holiness movement. In 1906 he rushed to Los Angeles to seek the baptism. He was not disappointed. He found the Azusa Street building overflowing with people speaking in tongues and worshiping God. After five days of prayer, Cashwell received the baptism.

He returned to Dunn where he called a special meeting in a tobacco warehouse, inviting people far and wide to hear his testimony. Vinson Synan in *The Old-Time Power* says, "The altars filled night after night and scores of people quickly received the pentecostal baptism and spoke in other tongues 'as the Spirit gave utterance.' It seemed that everyone was 'hungry' for the experience."[2]

Many of the Pentecostal Holiness preachers who received the baptism at Dunn returned to their churches to report what had happened. The experience repeated itself at the altars of church after church. As believers were added to the church, the denomination gravitated toward institutional methods to disciple men. Sunday school was used to teach members the Scriptures and ministers were enrolled in institutions of higher education.

Bishop C.H. Mason, founder of the Church of God in Christ, was drawn to Azusa Street by the news that reached his home in Memphis, Tennessee. After receiving the baptism, he stayed in Los Angeles five weeks before returning home. Arriving back in Memphis, he shared his experience and members of his holiness church received the baptism with tongues.

Pentecost had reached the Church of God in Christ, which was destined to become the largest black pentecostal denomination in America. By 1970 the church claimed a membership of one million and a worldwide constituency of three million in 10,000 churches.

Bishop Mason and his followers organized in what they said was the "authority of the Scriptures." They named a chief apostle (or general overseer), apostles, prophets, evangelists, pastors, elders, overseers, teachers, deacons, deaconesses and missionaries. These officials were assigned the responsibility of training new converts and guiding them in the ways of the Lord.

[2]Vinson Synan, *The Old-Time Power*, (Franklin Springs, Ga: Advocate Press, 1973), p. 109.

Although the Church of God (Cleveland, Tennesse) did not begin in the holiness movement, it subsequently became identified with it. Richard G. Spurling, a Baptist pastor in Monroe County, Tennesse, became concerned in 1884 over trends in his members' lives. He was unhappy with the lack of maturity in their lives. After trying to disciple people to Christ for two years without success, Spurling separated from the Baptist church in 1886, carrying seven people with him, including his son.

Calling themselves "The Christian Union," they eventually moved to Cherokee County, North Carolina, and formed a holiness church with another former Baptist group. The new Christian community sought God together until Pentecost came. A division in the church came in 1902 over the "tongues" issue. Those who opposed the experience left.

The church reorganized, naming an American Bible Society colporteur, A.J. Tomlinson, as pastor. He had visited the church over a seven-year period, warning they would err if they organized putting authority in the hands of men. Many pastors who received the baptism in the Holy Spirit in the Azusa Street revival united with the new movement. New churches were established under Tomlinson's leadership in Georgia and Tennessee, requiring further organization of the church with headquarters in Cleveland.

Tomlinson was made national overseer, a move which fulfilled his own prophetic warning about vesting too much authority in leadership. At the 1922 General Assembly, he asked for absolute authority in the denomination with power to personally select and appoint his National Council of Twelve Elders. He felt the Lord's sovereign rule over the church could only be realized if unconditional power were given to him. Tomlinson had to have that authority to bring the church into maturity.

The General Assembly refused, ordering an investigation of Tomlinson's activities instead. Fifteen charges were leveled against him, which led to his impeachment in 1923 by the National Court of Supreme Judges of the Church of God.

Tomlinson's efforts to bring the church to maturity through absolute authority split the denomination. Like those who would follow him in later discipleship movements, his motives were noble. Yet, having realized all other methods to develop character in believers had failed, he turned to "absolute authority" as a way of requiring change. In each case, demand for such authority vested in the pastor created division.

Milton A. Tomlinson separated with his disciples, forming the Church of God Prophecy with headquarters in Cleveland. Homer A. Tomlinson organized his followers into a third Church of God with headquarters in Queens Village, New York.

Efforts to disciple people through authoritative church government had proven disastrous in the Church of God. The church later named F.J. Lee as General Overseer and moved on to disciple believers through Bible schools, training centers and church colleges.

The Assemblies of God (General Council) is a prime example of pentecostal bodies moving rapidly to institutional methods to disciple new converts in Christian character. The denomination became the largest among classical pentecostal churches in the United States.

Formed in Hot Springs, Arkansas, in 1914 from a collection of new pentecostal churches and assemblies (although some of its leaders had been members of other denominations), it consisted mostly of Methodists who had joined the holiness movement. Bringing the holiness doctrine of "entire sanctification" with them, they established it as the basic doctrine around which members would be discipled. Many pastors expected the baptism in the Holy Spirit to destroy the believer's carnal mind, leaving him free to develop the character of Christ.

The Assemblies of God influenced classical pentecostalism to accept institutional methods to disciple their new converts. They established local congregations, with Bible study programs designed to form new habits in the disciple. A combined presbyterian and congregational form of church government was established to oversee their churches.

Institutions of higher learning were founded to train pastors and church leaders. Aggressive programs of evangelism and missions were adopted to convert the lost. By 1974 the church had 1,117,116 members in 69 countries throughout the world. While leaders were being trained in institutions, other "disciples" were enrolled in Sunday schools.

However, the gnawing need for men to come into community, to find a "place," was left untended. Again the stage had been set for radical discipleship to fill the void.

Scores of other small pentecostal denominations were formed. For the most part, they settled into the classical pentecostal mold like their larger brothers. Except for bringing the pentecostal experience of tongues back into the church, their programs and methods resembled other denominations in most respects. Discipleship training had been completely institutionalized.

Struggle with Secularism

World War I and the overthrow of the Russian monarchy in March, 1917, marked a turning point for the United States, which emerged as an industrial giant of the world. Young people were challenged by intellectualism. Marxist doctrine was discussed in the more intellectual circles. Many intellectuals said church people who believed in a personal Jesus as Savior were ignorant.

Pentecostal young people were embarrassed by the "emotionalism" of their parents. They were ridiculed in schools and looked upon as second-class citizens. People who prayed in tongues and shouted in churches were emotionally unbalanced, it was suggested. They were called "holy rollers."

Young people of all faiths—Catholic, Protestant, Jewish—found no challenge in the lifeless religion of their parents. Their plight was not helped by World War II. Nazism forced church leaders in Europe to support their atrocities or die. Those who believed in one true God seemed helpless. Confronted with these new ideologies, the American youth lost his identity with God. He lost his place. America was plunged into one of the greatest periods of anxiety and unrest since the Civil War.

Mass Evangelism–A Call to Discipleship

The same atmosphere which had ushered in the Great Awakening two hundred years before was ready again. Instead of German rationalism, French atheism and

English deism threatening the church's life, it was Marxist atheism, secular humanism and the social gospel. God's method of revival was the same, only the faces had changed.

Just as before when the church got bogged down in tradition, God sovereignly moved to bring forth anointed preachers like Billy Sunday. Then a number of "lesser lights"—some of them pentecostal—appeared. Finally, like a modern-day John the Baptist, Billy Graham attracted tens of thousands as he warned—first America, then the world—that impending doom was eminent if men did not abandon their godless behavior and humble themselves before their Maker.

Graham's anointed Los Angeles crusade of 1948 brought him to the attention of presidents and heads of state throughout the world. Thousands walked the aisles, accepting Jesus Christ as Lord and Savior. They were referred to existing denominational churches to be discipled.

The Southern Baptist evangelist clearly defined the way to peace and security. God was America's only hope, he declared. Religious and secular life, black and white, was on the threshold of the greatest test in American history, according to Graham. In short, he called America to find her *place* in God.

However, Graham did little to call men into personal discipleship for the purpose of training and service. This was picked up by organizations such as the Navigators, Campus Crusade for Christ and Inter-Varsity Christian Fellowship, who demanded strict disciplines of followers.

Black America Rejects White Discipleship
The shaking of the nation's foundation—just as Graham

predicted—began in the mid-1950's. Martin Luther King, Jr., (1929-1968) was pastor of the Dexter Avenue Baptist Church in Montgomery, Alabama, when he was thrust into the role of social justice crusader. He formed the Southern Christian Leadership Conference to demand equal justice for blacks.

King led black America to test the strength of every segregated institution—from secular universities to Christian churches. Before it was over, the integrity of Christian character in practically every church would be challenged.

The eloquence of the fiery, Southern-born preacher swept the black man into dreams of receiving his share of the world's goods now. Disciples were recruited to King by the thousands, demanding their rightful place in a Christian culture. But the assassin's bullet which killed King in 1968 shocked blacks into reality. Taking their place in American life would be harder than they thought. Violence splintered militant black communities. Christian militants developed a new "black theology" which declared Jesus was black.

Dr. James H. Cone, black associate professor of theology at Union Theological Seminary in New York City, said, "Whether whites want to hear it or not, Christ is black, baby, with all the features which are so detestable to white society."[3]

Another militant black religious faction rejected Christian doctrine completely. Elijah Poole, born to a black Georgia sharecropper, announced that "Allah," god of the Nation of Islam, had made him head of the black man in America. Poole changed his name to Elijah

[3]Gerald S. Snyder, "The Religious Reawakening in America," (U.S. News & World Report, Inc., Washington, D.C., 1972) p. 109.

Muhammad. Militant black disciples rapidly submitted to his authority, increasing its ranks to some 100,000 members.

The teachings of Jesus did nothing to change a man's life, the Black Muslims said. Muhammad, true holy prophet of Allah, had shown the black man of Africa a better way before the white man introduced Jesus to America. The black man had traced roots back to an African culture and identified with it. He had found a new place in life, but lost it with Jesus Christ.

Even the black Christians who stayed in their established churches did not escape the unrest of their generation. Hundreds of black pastors took up the revolutionary teachings of Martin Luther King. They called their people to become responsible and take their place in American society.

Efforts to integrate the churches uncovered a cesspool of unresolved conflict deep within Christians. Modern discipleship training had failed to change the inner character of many believers.

Young people were confused by the picture their parents painted. They spoke of love for the brethren in one breath and cried "nigger" or "honkey" in the next. Young people said the church had failed. Like the Hindu mystic, Ghandi, most people confessed they had no problem with Jesus. It was His disciples they couldn't stand.

The Search of the Sixties

The war in Viet Nam reflected many of the flaws in America. The intellectualism of the humanists, the social reforms of the Marxists and the church's discipleship hadn't delivered what they promised. A frantic search for reality in the untouched supernatural world began.

Rebelling against the hypocrisies of their Christian fathers caused many young people to lose their identity in life. While white young people embraced Eastern religions such as Hare Krishna and Yoga, blacks were rushing to Muslim temples. Many of both races dropped off into occult worship. Others searched for a better world through hard drugs. Timothy Leary, a college professor, said they could "tune in" through LSD.

The Jesus Movement

A spiritual revolution was taking place at the same time. Many young people were hungry for a vital experience with Jesus Christ. Rejecting the hypocritical lives of many in the established churches, these new believers paid homage to Christ outside the church.

The main emphasis of the Jesus movement, which flourished from 1967 to 1972, was on discipleship. The converts believed that Jesus was alive and calling disciples to himself. Jesus was the common denominator of everything they did. They accepted the Bible as the Word of God, searching it daily for answers to all their problems. They taught that each person could have a vital and personal experience with Christ.

The Holy Spirit was considered vital to the believer's experience. Emphasis upon the infilling of the Holy Spirit laid the ground work for future identification with the charismatic renewal. Many found a cure for drugs, alcohol and illicit sex through the power of the Holy Spirit.

Some opportunists rose among groups of "Jesus

people," leading them into extremes of community life and submission. Counterculture communes and communities came into prominence, quickly adopting various forms of authority over the young disciples. Some were balanced scripturally. Others moved off into extremes, with the new converts accepting absolute authority from their leaders. The latter groups generally ended up out of balance scripturally. A few were led away as disciples of Sun Myung Moon of the Unification Church, David "Moses" Berg of the Children of God and others.

Formation of Charismatic Churches

At the same time genuine restoration movements—some in denominations, some separate—began to spring up. Mennonite pastor Gerald Derstine and his church experienced a special visitation of the Holy Spirit in December, 1954, in Minnesota. The experience, which lasted seven days, moved Derstine out of the shelter of his Mennonite denomination into a new world.

In time, Derstine developed two Christian retreat centers, one at Bradenton, Florida, and another at Ogema, Minnesota, for the teaching of charismatic laity within various denominations. He also established a special school of ministry to train young men and women.

Other new churches, some only called "fellowships," sprang up as charismatics from various prayer groups clustered around men who became their pastors. Many such fellowships were ecumenical in nature because their members came from so many different denominations. Efforts were made to disciple men on a local level, clinging to the sovereignty of the local church under local apostolic authority.

Renewal in Mainline Churches

Renewal penetrating mainline churches brought a demand for discipleship programs within the denominations. London-born Dennis Bennett, for ten years rector of the 2,600-member St. Mark's Episcopal Church in Van Nuys, California, shocked the ecumenical world on April 3, 1960. That Sunday morning Bennett told his congregation he had been baptized in the Holy Spirit and spoke in tongues. He later was forced to resign.

Time, Newsweek and major newspapers carried Bennett's story. "Tongues" had reached the most prestigious churches in America. Almost simultaneously, as if God were personally directing the march, the experience repeated itself in hundreds of churches. Pastors and church members alike shared similar stories of being filled with "new wine."

Reactions from church authorities varied. Catholic and Episcopal bishops made room for the new charismatics, calling for discipleship programs designed to develop those caught up in the renewal. Other authorities were reactionary, sometimes "disfellowshiping" charismatics completely.

After Bennett's bishop reassigned him to another parish (St. Luke's in Seattle, Washington), renewal in Episcopal circles found greater acceptance. Episcopalians generally followed the methods of the Catholics— planning conferences, entering community life and encouraging renewal within the church.

Lutherans, Presbyterians and Methodists joined the swelling ranks of denominations embracing the renewal. Jews by the hundreds were converted and baptized in the Holy Spirit. They formed Christian Messianic Fellowships dedicated to introducing Jesus Christ as Messiah to other Jews. Programs were established to train new recruits to evangelize.

Formation of Communities

In February, 1967, four Catholics at Duquesne University in Pittsburgh were baptized in the Holy Spirit. A few days later several students joined the faculty members in a weekend retreat. They too received. Kevin Ranaghan and his wife, Dorothy, who would become leaders in the Catholic renewal, were part of the group.

Steve Clark and Ralph Martin, who had been in the Americanized-Spanish Cursillo movement, received. They became leaders in the new Catholic charismatic communities, the largest of which is the Word of God Community at Ann Arbor, Michigan.

Clark wrote *Building Christian Communities* in 1972, offering guidelines for the structure of basic Christian communities. Believers, searching for relief from the "lawless" society, turned to Christian communities to find spiritual authority, love and family life. Reformers called for churches to be restructured to meet the needs of their members.

Howard A. Snyder in *The Problem of Wine Skins* wrote, "The Body Church . . . holds no property and needs none. It arranges its worship gatherings according to available space in homes, schools, rented halls or other facilities. Its structure is largely organic, based on a network of small groups bound together by large-group corporate worship experiences."[4]

Brethren living together in communes and communities like the ones suggested by Snyder all called for changes in the basic structure of church life. By 1978 networks of communities stretched across the length and breadth of the United States. They were represented by such large communities as the 1,500-member Word of God Community in Ann Arbor to the small Mennonite Fellowship of Hope community of some 90 people in Elkhart, Indiana. Some communities pool all their resources, while others permit each family unit to oversee its own income while sharing with others as needs arise. Problems remained, however, as the people's dreams failed to materialize. Those who chose to live in communities continued to struggle with pressures in personal relationships and resentments toward strong, authoritative leaders.

Organizations Aiding the Renewal

Many discipleship organizations which developed on the college campuses of America strengthened the interest in discipleship. These para-church organizations were all evangelistic. They centered on Bible study for effective discipleship, and all stated they existed to support the established churches.

The best known among these groups is probably Dr. Bill Bright's Campus Crusade for Christ, based in Arrowhead Springs, California. They gathered disciples throughout the world who studied Bible courses on salvation, the Spirit-filled life and commitment.

The Navigators, founded by the late Dawson Trottman, produced materials grounding thousands of

[4]Howard A. Snyder, *The Problem of Wine Skins*, (Downers Grove, Ill: Inter-Varsity Press, 1977), p. 75.

new disciples in the Scriptures. Simplified methods were adopted and distributed throughout the world to teach disciples how to memorize the Bible. Navigator groups were formed in schools and the military service. They were committed to introducing people to Jesus Christ and establishing the converts in the Bible.

Inter-Varsity Christian Fellowship was another group that had a wide impact on the college campus. IVCF operated on a Bible study and fellowship basis. It also opened a publishing house.

Yokefellow groups, loosely organized by Quaker teacher Elton Trueblood, were formed in prisons, aiding in the conversion of many. Once converted to Christ, these groups banded together to "share their inner feelings" in small groups.

Mass Lay Evangelism

When Demos Shakarian and five other men formed the Full Gospel Business Men's Fellowship International in 1953, the stage was set for one of the most extensive lay renewal movements in history. Filling a void which its earlier counterpart, the Christian Businessmen's Committee, had recognized but failed to meet because of its insistence on denying the gifts of the Spirit as valid, the FGBMFI held monthly meetings and began to establish chapters throughout the world.

Downtown restaurants were used for dinner meetings, where prominent businessmen gave their testimonies. Professional and business men were invited to hear others tell how they had been "born again." Many testified to being baptized in the Holy Spirit with the gift of tongues. Others told of being healed supernaturally of diseases.

Regional, national and international conventions were held, where thousands listened to Bible teachings and personal testimonies.

FGBMFI board of directors were eventually enlarged to include businessmen, lawyers, physicians and educators. They dedicated themselves to converting the lost and getting them filled with the Holy Spirit.

Discipleship Training Restored

Swelling membership in charismatic circles demanded that preachers and teachers devote themselves to the training of new disciples. Many of the new charismatic churches and fellowships were unprepared to train new converts.

Like churches of previous generations, leaders saw the need to establish institutions to develop leadership. Bible schools and colleges were founded to meet the growing need.

Melodyland School of Theology, Oral Roberts University, Liberty Bible College, Rhema Bible Institute, Christ for the Nations Institute, Gospel Crusade School of Ministry, Gloryland Bible Institute and many other schools were established. Pat Robertson of Christian Broadcasting Network and Jim Bakker of the PTL Club also founded schools. History was repeating itself.

A Coming Together

Many charismatics throughout the United States found common ground for fellowship in the ministry of Christian Growth Ministries at Ft. Lauderdale, Florida. Five nationally known Bible teachers were represented in the teaching team of Derek Prince, Bob Mumford, Charles Simpson, Don Basham and Ern Baxter. These men were the charismatic evangelists—recruiting thousands into the charismatic movement.

Hundreds gathered in convocations to study as the CGM teachers expounded on such subjects as "Divine Order in the Home," "Personal Relationships," "The Kingdom of God," "Personal Restoration," "Commitment, Covenant and Community," "Practical Discipleship," and "Demonology."

Annual convocations were held across the nation. Families came, enrolling children in special classes. Large classes were held for every age group, dealing with various Bible subjects related to the Christian life. Sessions were held where large numbers of people were baptized in the Holy Spirit with the manifestation of tongues.

Doctrinal Conflict with Classical Pentecostals

New doctrinal positions—notably those on demonology—created conflict with the older pentecostal churches who were trying to understand their new charismatic neighbors. American pentecostals had formed their theology from Wesley's doctrine of sanctification, only experiencing tongues after the Azusa Street revival.

According to Latourette, "Wesley's main themes were conscious acceptance with God and daily growth in holiness."[5] Yet his doctrine of sanctification was later taken to mean that the carnal nature was completely destroyed in an act of sanctification.

"Entire sanctification frees the believer from inbred

[5]Latourette, op. cit., p. 1025.

sin," wrote Stephen S. White in the *Five Cardinal Elements in the Doctrine of Entire Sanctification*. "The old man or the carnal mind is eradicated and not merely suppressed or counteracted. Holiness is imparted—and not merely imputed—to the saved when he is entirely sanctified."[6]

Classical pentecostals had problems with the new practice of casting demons out of born-again, Spirit-filled disciples of Jesus Christ. They said it was impossible, explaining that God had cleansed the body of the believer in sanctification and no other spirit could reside there.

Pentecostal pastors warned their members to stay away from the new charismatics. Basham, an ordained minister in the Disciples of Christ church, responded by writing a book, *Can A Christian Have A Demon?* The book contained Scriptures proving, he said, that a demon could inhabit the body of a Christian.

Basham and Prince, who was educated in Britain as a scholar at Eton College and King's College, Cambridge, joined in teaching on such subjects as "Deliverance," "Restraining and Casting Down Satan" and "Spiritual Weapons: The Blood, The Word, Our Testimony."

The Call for Authority

Christian Growth Ministries called a "Shepherd's Conference" in March, 1973, at Leesburg, Florida, to call for order and authority in the renewal. Many recognized the need to give spiritual guidance to the thousands of new, enthusiastic charismatics who were floating from one meeting to another, talking about their dynamic relationship with Jesus Christ.

Yet some of the charismatics were looking toward

[6]Stephen S. White, *Five Cardinal Elements in the Doctrine of Entire Sanctification*, (Kansas City, Mo: Beacon Hill Press, 1949), p. 43.

teaching seminars, regional conferences and FGBMFI meetings as "substitute churches." There was a tendency to abandon New Testament concepts of the local church. Organizations founded to support the Christian church—such as FGBMFI—sometimes appeared to lose sight of their mission, becoming para-churches instead. Many people were satisfied with "electronic" churches, receiving all their Christian fellowship and instruction from television.

Charismatic leaders across the country recognized a need for order and authority as the ranks of the renewal swelled. Many people—especially those young in the Lord—needed leadership and discipline over their lives. And as charismatic churches grew up, some almost overnight, there was a genuine need to fellowship with brothers of like mind.

On March 3, Derek Prince set the tone of the meeting with a scholarly teaching on the "Relationship of Apostles and Elders to the Local Church."

"If I speak about what I am going to speak about now," Prince said, "I am going ahead of my experience and I think ahead of the experience of all of us here. . . . I am going to preach today on something that none of us have yet fully entered into though I believe we're right on the threshold of it."

He then developed historically the birth and growth of the primitive church in the New Testament, showing the development of church government, both local and extra-local, as he saw it. Prince's teaching was balanced by that of Pastor Ken Sumrall who taught that the local church should be the highest authority in the Kingdom. He indicated the five-fold ministries were working well in the local church in Pensacola, Florida.

The following year a nationwide "Shepherd's Conference" was held in Montreat, North Carolina. This, too, was sponsored by CGM teachers, who enlisted other select men to join them in a steering committee. At this conference—attended by more than 2,000 men from across the nation—extra-local submission and the submission of a "sheep's" will to the shepherd were promoted as "God's new wave of anointing."

The shepherd's movement was underway.

Influence from Argentina

While many in the new charismatic churches expected leaders to develop concepts of church government along the lines given at the Leesburg conference, the strongest imput for new methods of discipleship came from Juan Carlos Ortiz, who had developed a program in Argentina.

Considered to be effective in developing disciples, Ortiz was invited to the United States to explain the methods employed in his country. His visit in October of 1973 was considered by many an opportunity to learn how to bring Christian men to maturity.

Problems existed in the charismatic renewal. Many people were more interested in the supernatural power of the Holy Spirit than in accepting discipline over their lives. Leaders were looking for ways to bring the new charismatics into maturity. Character development was lagging behind the use of charismatic gifts—creating problems like those in the Corinthian church (1 Cor. 12-14). Discipleship methods developed in Argentina seemed to offer the best solution to the problem.

Interestingly, the book, *Call To Discipleship*, issued a

warning in the foreword to anyone who might want to duplicate Ortiz's methods. Few heeded the warning.

Discipleship Methods and Church Government Merged
Charles Simpson, a former Southern Baptist pastor and a teacher with CGM, had become discouraged with charismatics who floated from one meeting to another without coming under any discipline. He felt they were not interested in developing mature Christian character.

To achieve his goals, Simpson called men to develop submitted relationships with each other. Each man was asked to submit to another as his shepherd. Cooperating shepherds submitted one to another in a pyramiding fashion throughout the charismatic movement.

Correction of a brother would be easy to accomplish. It would be directed to the leading shepherd over his group of submitted shepherds. That high-ranking shepherd would then pass the rule of discipline down the line through each submitted shepherd until the brother in question was disciplined.

"A man entering into such a commitment deserves to receive teachings which are not available to just anyone," according to Simpson. The free-floating people would not be privileged to receive certain revelations. They would only be given to shepherds in submitted relationships.

Simpson believed that his plan would enforce character changes in his disciples. In that way, a charismatic could remain in his denominational church but would still have to accept the authority of his shepherd over his life. His tithe would go to the shepherd, not his church.

In return, the shepherd would give personal supervision in the development of his Christian character.

The shepherd would also be available twenty-four hours a day. As the disciple accepted the shepherd's spiritual authority over his life, goals in character development would be achieved.

Another member of the CGM teaching team, Bob Mumford, began teaching on the one-to-one relationships of sheep (or church members) to shepherds (or pastors) in seminars throughout the country. "Every sheep needs to find his shepherd and submit to him," Mumford taught.

Many persons who heard the teachings felt compelled to find a shepherd who would oversee and direct their lives. Some relationships were cemented locally. Others were formed extra-locally.

Even pastors of large denominational churches accepted a shepherd's authority while maintaining a dual relationship with their own denominational hierarchy. Relationships with other men from the national council down through the country were developed on a one-to-one basis.

Simultaneously, many new prayer groups and fellowships throughout the country were growing into full-size churches, adopting various forms of established local church government to meet their needs. Most of the local churches remained independent of each other. Pastors and leaders not in the shepherdship movement began to call for extra-local meetings, where fellowship among the brethren could be restored. The move of the CGM teachers into rigid forms of discipleship had left a void in national leadership for many charismatic groups whose pastors did not enter the shepherdship movement.

Several "summit meetings" were called to try to resolve the issues. And while the CGM teachers toned down their radical public call to discipleship, the charismatic movement was splintered in confusion and distrust.

Charismatic Rifts

From its beginning in 1973, the issue of discipleship as defined by CGM was controversial. "Shepherdship" conferences were held periodically after 1973—at Montreat, North Carolina, and Atlanta—with CGM teachers in leadership. Each conference became more exclusive as it went along, giving greater emphasis to the new teachings and direction from CGM.

By mid-August, 1975, the controversy was becoming heated. Thirty of the nation's best-known charismatic leaders gathered in Minneapolis to thrash out problems stemming from the new discipleship movement. Then Pat Robertson of CBN and Kathryn Kuhlman publicly renounced the concepts of submission and discipleship taught by the shepherdship teachers. Various officials of FGBMFI also took issue with the teachings.

Efforts to establish discipline within the charismatic renewal by sealing men to men in one-on-one submission had polarized charismatic leaders into various camps. History had again repeated itself.

There was one major difference, however. This time all the participants, both those calling for strong concepts of discipleship and those opposing, were Spirit-baptized brothers. Their access to the Holy Spirit left the possibility open for not only reconciliation, but a deeper revelation of God's word to His people than ever before realized. Could it be possible that this conflict, pitting brother against brother, was God's method to ferret out truth and have it applied to the Kingdom in a new dimension?

6 | *Character Goals for Kingdom Living*

As I continued my study of discipleship, I decided to make a fresh study of *what* Jesus taught His disciples. It is the Word that will change a person—not how the Word is taught.

That was it!

If believers could be brought to the place where they could "hear" the Word of God, that Living Word would supernaturally change their lives. "For the word of God is living and active and sharper than any two-edged sword," according to Hebrews 4:12 (NASB).

"The words that I have spoken to you are spirit and are life," Jesus told His grumbling disciples (John 6:63 NASB). Every word God speaks is revelation. That is, it is an unveiling of His life and personality.

Jesus later told the Father, "For the words which Thou gavest Me I have given to them; and they received them, and truly understood that I came forth from Thee, and they believed that Thou didst send Me" (John 17:8 NASB).

The Lord Jesus Christ taught His disciples to listen to His words. They came from God—for in Jesus Christ, God was speaking.

Abraham found his place with God by hearing the word of the Lord and obeying it. Jesus did the same with His disciples. He taught them the word of the Father. He gave them opportunities to practice their faith. He let them observe His ministry. He taught them to love and respect each other (John 13:34-35).

Finally, Jesus instructed them, "These things I have spoken to you, while abiding with you. But the Helper, the Holy Spirit, whom the Father will send in My Name, He will teach you all things, and bring to your remembrance all that I said to you" (John 14:25-26 NASB).

Even after He had ascended into heaven, Jesus had made provision for His disciples. They would continue hearing the word of God until those very words produced the life and maturity of Jesus in them.

The Sermon on the Mount

In the calling of the twelve disciples (Matt. 9:9, Mark 1:16-20, Luke 5:1-11), Jesus had assembled a ragtag assortment of men—political rebels, fishermen, a tax collector and the like. They were people with character flaws, hot tempers and bad habits. Judas Iscariot had a problem with money.

In correcting these flaws, Jesus knew that well-balanced, stable and mature men of God would come forth. However, the Lord recognized this God-given character would not be developed overnight. It would come as a gradual process during His earthly ministry, and then be further developed after His Ascension with the Holy Spirit as the teacher.

In studying the life and teachings of Jesus in relation to His twelve disciples, it is clear that the Lord was less interested in methods of instruction than in bringing twelve "unlearned" men into Christian maturity.

The heart of the Lord's overall message to His disciples is found in chapters five, six and seven of Matthew, commonly known as the "Sermon on the Mount." It was this message followed by an intense three-year period of practical application that prepared the disciples for their job of spreading the gospel into all the world.

Contrary to popular opinion, the Sermon on the Mount was not delivered just once. Since it was His basic message to the disciples, Jesus presented it over and over. This is demonstrated by Matthew's choice of words in chapter five, verse two. "And opening His mouth He began to teach them. . . ."

The King James Version says, "And he opened his mouth, and taught them. . . ." If the KJV were correct, it would mean Jesus delivered the teachings one time and never again.

However, the New American Standard Bible is much closer to the original language of the text. With the use of the imperfect verb tense, "taught," Matthew shows that Jesus was in the habit of teaching His disciples in this manner. The imperfect tense in the original language denotes habitual, continuous action in the past. Thus, Jesus gave the Sermon at one sitting and repeated its contents many times thereafter.

The Message Given in Public

"And seeing the multitudes, he went up into a

mountain: and when he was set, his disciples came unto him" (Matt. 5:1).

Although Jesus was speaking to the disciples, He was within speaking distance of the multitudes. No effort was made to exclude anyone from hearing what He taught. Matthew 7:28 points out at the conclusion of this first teaching session, "the *people* were astonished at his doctrine." The NASB says "the *multitudes* were amazed at His teaching."

One of the basic principles of the teaching ministry of Jesus is that He never said anything in secret that could not be said in public. There were times when He explained parables to the disciples in private after He had spoken them in the open—but He never gave secret teachings.

By His own words in John 18:20, this point is well established. Jesus was on trial and the high priest was questioning Him about His disciples and His teaching. "Jesus answered him, 'I have spoken openly to the world; I always taught in synagogues, and in the temple, where all the Jews come together; and I spoke nothing in secret' " (NASB).

I believe the Lord meant exactly what He said. He spoke nothing in secret. In fact, anyone who says God has given a special word—reserved for a privileged few but not available for the body of Christ—does not understand this basic principle of the life and ministry of Jesus Christ.

In explaining His parables to the disciples (Mark 4:11-12), Jesus acknowledged a certain uniqueness about the Word of God. "To you has been given the mystery of the kingdom of God; but those who are outside get everything in parables, in order that while seeing, they may see and not perceive; and while hearing, they may hear and not understand; lest they return again and be forgiven" (NASB).

The Lord declared that the Word of God had a mystery built within it. It will minister life and strength to those who receive it by faith and it will become a stumbling block to those who would abuse it. In effect, He showed the Word can be shared in an open manner and still accomplish all that God intended (see Isaiah 55:11).

Jesus never operated in any fashion that showed signs of elitism or sectarianism. On the contrary, He broke into human history to break down barriers between God and man. This was true during the Lord's earthly ministry and it is true today in this great outpouring of the Holy Spirit. The Lord is drawing believers together, breaking down sectarian walls. He is not separating His family members. He is bringing them together.

The "Beatitudes"

The word "beatitude" is not one found in the Bible. It is a word that has been coined to refer to a particular literary form used in Scripture. The Interpreter's Bible says, "The Beatitude begins with the word 'blessed' and constitutes a declaration of praise in which rewards are promised for moral attitudes and behavior that become the Christian."

For instance, Psalm 1 is a beatitude. "Blessed is the man that walketh not in the counsel of the ungodly, nor standeth in the way of sinners, nor sitteth in the seat of the scornful." Beatitudes are found in both Old and New Testament.

As Jesus listed these various beatitudes (Matt. 5:3-12), there appears a progression showing the development of

Christian character in the disciple's life. It's almost as if the Beatitudes lay out the totality of the Christian life—from the first moment a person opens his life to Christ until the very end of his earthly existence.

The King James Version shows that the Beatitudes all begin, "Blessed are." The word "are" is italicized showing that it does not appear in the Greek text. This leads us to believe Jesus did not say "blessed are." But, he was saying, "There is bliss and there is joy in this way of life, in this attitude."

"Blessed are the poor in spirit"

The first beatitude (Matt. 5:3) says, "Blessed are the poor in spirit: for theirs is the kingdom of heaven."

The last beatitude (Matt. 5:10-12) offers the same reward. "Blessed are they which are persecuted for righteousness' sake: for theirs is the kingdom of heaven.

"Blessed are ye, when men shall revile you, and persecute you, and shall say all manner of evil against you falsely, for my sake. Rejoice, and be exceeding glad: for great is your reward in heaven: for so persecuted they the prophets which were before you."

The first and the last beatitudes are the only ones which list the same reward for the disciple: "theirs is the kingdom of heaven." By listing them in that sequence, Jesus demonstrated there was something basic about a disciple's attitude toward God that never changed. The disciple would always feel a sense of helplessness and total dependence upon the Holy Spirit. It is this attitude of total reliance upon God which gives the disciple understanding of how the Kingdom operates.

A person who is "poor in spirit" is one who realizes his

spiritual destitution in his relationship with God. Because a person sees himself helpless without God, he moves forward placing his confidence in the Savior. That's essentially what happens at conversion. A person realizes his helplessness in this life and places his trust in God through the person of Jesus Christ.

That is the starting point in the Christian experience. However, after progressing through various stages of development, Jesus showed, the disciple comes back to the same point. The disciple begins the Christian life in a state of helplessness. He ends it in the same condition. The Scripture shows the reward is identical—"for theirs is the kingdom of heaven."

There is, of course, a mountain of difference between helplessness and hopelessness. Many people confuse these attitudes. Hopelessness contains desperation and futility. Many problems look hopeless.

Helpless means a person is defenseless or powerless. It encourages trust in God—for many times He alone can solve the pressing dilemmas of life. It is a basic part of a Christian's "walk in the Spirit."

I did not understand this attitude of helplessness until several years ago, as a Southern Baptist pastor, I found myself before my 40-man board of deacons listening to the reading of a list of charges against me. Like Jesus, I was guilty as charged and I couldn't offer a word in defense. Admittedly, there were half-truths in the accusations but the charges were basically true. I was guilty.

The board chairman intoned, "According to our information, you believe after a person is saved he can have a second experience known as the 'baptism of the Holy Spirit' and can pray in unknown tongues."

I couldn't argue with that. I knew it was true from the Scriptures. I had even experienced it personally while in prayer. Thus I was guilty as charged.

Another statement was read: "The other night you went over to an elderly man's house. You anointed him with oil, laid hands on him, saying, 'Be healed in the name of Jesus.' This accusation says you think you're a faith healer and that you have the power to heal."

There was a half-truth in the latter statements. Yet there was enough truth that I was still guilty. How could I say I'm not a faith healer but I believe Jesus Christ is, and He expects His disciples to carry on this work in His name?

Those are just light persecutions. But for the first time in my life, I felt the meaning of Matthew 5:3, 10-12. I was absolutely helpless—guilty as charged.

I have since discovered a person who has received the Holy Spirit and tasted of God's supernatural gifts can easily revert back to relying upon himself. A person with natural charisma can move from under the anointing of the Holy Spirit into his own natural talents. Many people won't know the difference.

Why then did Jesus teach that helplessness was a part of the mature life? He wanted His disciples to understand this vital difference between helplessness and hopelessness. A hopeless person has no faith. A helpless person can learn to trust God in every circumstance.

Jesus wanted His disciples to be people who always relied on the Spirit of God. "Theirs is the kingdom of heaven," he declared. That's where kingdom living is. It is absolute and total reliance on God in every situation. Thus a disciple is helpless apart from God. Regardless of a

Christian's maturity, he will always live with the feeling of helplessness—having to totally rely upon God.

"Blessed are those who mourn"

Matthew 5:4 says, "Blessed are they that mourn: for they shall be comforted."

It's interesting that Jesus introduced this beatitude right after teaching His disciples the necessity of realizing their helplessness. Mourning is a funeral word. It represents a "deep groaning" that takes place, for instance, in a person who has suddenly lost a close friend in death. For a Christian, it's the dying of the flesh, or the "old man."

Jesus taught this attitude was necessary for His disciples. It is an attitude toward sin. The Bill Ligon translation of that verse reads, "Blessed are those who have a mourning attitude toward sin, for they shall be comforted."

When a person reaches the point where his heart is heavy toward the world's sin—his own and those of people around him—then the Holy Spirit can greatly use that person. Isaiah had reached that point. Listen to the old prophet's lamentation: "Woe is me, for I am ruined! Because I am a man of unclean lips, And I live among a people of unclean lips; For my eyes have seen the King, the Lord of hosts" (Isa. 6:5 NASB).

This attitude of mourning over sin will permit a person to be obedient to the words of James 5:19-20. "My brethren, if any among you strays from the truth, and one turns him back, let him know that he who turns a sinner from the error of his way will save his soul from death, and will cover a multitude of sins" (NASB).

The Holy Spirit often deals with my wife and me, as the parents of two active teen-age sons, about sin in our children's lives. Because the Holy Spirit functions in this way, we can then exercise the proper discipline with our boys. If we didn't have this mourning attitude about sin, we might overlook their misbehavior, permitting bad habits to form and hindering the development of their Christian character.

In using the word "comforted" to describe the reward of those who have a right attitude about sin, Jesus described the work of the Holy Spirit. In John 16:7 He used the noun form of the same word to denote the Holy Spirit (*paracletos*). The word means "one who draws alongside to help." He is the "Holy Comforter."

Thus Jesus showed His disciples as they drew closer to God in repentance for sin the Holy Spirit, by virtue of His office, would comfort and strengthen them.

When the Holy Spirit operates in this way, a disciple should have a right attitude about the sin in his life. The right attitude is one of continual repentance.

A follower of Jesus Christ should expect this attitude to be present all the days of his life. He will walk in victory and joy while carrying within himself the ability to repent over sin when he confronts it.

Of course, this is not condemnation. That is a work of the devil. A mourning attitude toward sin should lead the disciple to repentance, and repentance brings forgiveness (1 John 1:9).

Followers of the Lord Jesus need to accept this mourning attitude toward sin as a part of their daily Christian walk. This attitude will not make a believer somber or "down in the mouth." It will permit Christians to blush again. That is a good quality in one's character.

Alexander Pope wrote many years ago about the sultry work of sin:

"Vice is a monster of so frightful mien,
As to be hated, needs to be seen;
Yet seen too oft, familiar with her face,
We first endure, then pity, then embrace."

Christians are confronted daily with situations that no longer cause them to blush. Yet these same situations would have caused our forefathers to hang their heads in shame. Already God's people are conditioned to accept sin in many situations, instead of having a mourning attitude toward it.

In a recent Associated Press story Marilyn Marshall, the last stripper to dance at a Philadelphia burlesque house before it was closed, said: "Television and porno movies killed us. What you can see on TV now is what these people used to come here to see."

As soon as sin or the temptation to sin comes into a disciple's life, the Holy Spirit will give him a right attitude about that sin. No one else will have to tell him what is right or wrong. The Holy Spirit will take the Word of God and show a disciple where there is sin. Teaching new converts this principle is the best discipling one can do.

An architect in our church told me recently that God had shown him many of the concepts used to succeed in his profession had become sin in his life. "The Lord showed me an aggressive, determined attitude of imposing my will over another person, requiring him to accept my product, whether needed or not, was sin," the architect said. Because of that, he had to throw out many of his books on salesmanship.

In my own life that happened. While I was a Southern Baptist missionary to Spain, the Holy Spirit showed me the same principles I used to build churches could be used in the secular world just as effectively. I was relying on methods and personal abilities.

Jesus said to me, "That's sin. I want you to repent of it. Except I build the house, it is built in vain."

"Blessed are the gentle"

"Blessed are the meek: for they shall inherit the earth," says Matthew 5:5. The New American Standard Bible uses the word "gentle" in place of "meek." Of course, meekness does not mean weakness. On the contrary, this word describes a person who is well-trained and obedient.

The story of the dog trainer perfectly illustrates this beatitude. The trainer takes a dog and teaches him to fetch a thrown stick. After being trained in this manner, the man throws a stick but does not command "fetch." If the dog goes after the stick, that's habit. If the dog remains in position until the command is given, that's obedience or genuine meekness.

Thus Jesus was demonstrating to His disciples the importance of being obedient. There are many Christians who have failed to plug into this truth. Some have moved out too rapidly in ministry while the Lord was saying "stay and learn." Others have lounged around the church house for years never learning to go out and "fetch."

Jesus taught that obedient disciples "shall inherit the earth." They shall literally inherit the land. In essence, Jesus said, "Those who are obedient inherit all they are supposed to receive."

John 15:7-8 bears out this promise. "If you abide in Me,

and My words abide in you, ask whatever you wish, and it shall be done for you. By this is My Father glorified, that you bear much fruit, and so prove to be My disciples" (NASB).

The disciple who discovers how to receive his inheritance from God learns that this process begins in obedience. This is a consistent principle from Genesis to Revelation. God blesses obedience and He punishes disobedience.

The story of Joseph is a prime example of God's blessing through obedience. Sold into slavery through the deception of his brothers, Joseph found himself living in the house of Potiphar, an officer of Pharaoh and captain of the guard. Potiphar's wife tried to seduce Joseph and the young Israelite ended up in jail. But Joseph stayed true to God. In the end, of course, he became governor over all the land of Egypt, second in command to Pharaoh himself.

Joseph had found a unique truth about God—stay obedient to the eternal Lord and His blessings will follow you. "All these blessings shall come on thee, and overtake thee, if thou shalt hearken unto the voice of the Lord thy God" (Deut. 28:2).

The Christian who locks into this dynamic principle of God has plugged himself into the Source of unlimited blessing and provision. Thus when the Lord says forgive, the disciple of Christ forgives. When the Lord says bless, the disciple blesses. Whatever the Lord says, the disciple does—fully knowing it will bring reward.

"Blessed are those who hunger and thirst . . ."
"Blessed are they which do hunger and thirst after righteousness: for they shall be filled," says Matthew 5:6.

This type of hunger and thirst is the kind a man experiences when his life hangs between starvation and rescue. That man knows he will die unless someone comes to his aid or he finds food and water.

Every believer should realize that hungering and thirsting for righteousness will bring an infilling. Yet—after that same believer is filled—he will experience hunger and thirst at various times. This attitude, then, will be present with a disciple of Jesus Christ as he walks through this life.

A believer must continue to hunger and thirst *after* Jesus. This, of course, is a paradox. How can a man be hungry and filled at the same time? I have experienced that physically. At times, I've had an emptiness inside. I tried to feed my stomach even though I wasn't hungry physically. I have learned from such experiences that this feeling is often hunger in my spirit, not my stomach.

It was this experience of hungering and thirsting for righteousness that brought my wife and myself to recognize our need for the baptism with the Holy Spirit. We discovered something was missing in our lives while serving on the mission field in Spain—even though we had succeeded in large pastorates in the United States.

Our tradition ignored the baptism of the Holy Spirit and speaking in tongues as a valid experience for today. Yet the hunger and thirst inside of us became so intense, we sought after Jesus in desperation. In seeking after Him, we both were filled—with the Holy Spirit. The experience revolutionized our lives and ministry.

Many people seek the gifts and power of the Holy Spirit when they need only seek after one thing—Jesus Christ. Altars fill up many times with people seeking "more power." They don't need more power. They simply need Him. In seeking and receiving Him, all the gifts and fruit of the Spirit are part of the package.

"Blessed are the merciful"

"Blessed are the merciful: for they shall obtain mercy," says Matthew 5:7.

This kind of mercy is not pity or a condescending attitude toward someone in need. This "mercy" is an action word. It is the kind that permits one person to see through the eyes of another. This "mercy" enables a disciple to put on another's shoes and understand his feelings in the light of his needs and problems.

Critical judgment is one of the greatest temptations in the life of a Spirit-filled believer. It can sour a Christian's relationship with the Lord quicker than anything else outside of the six danger areas (to be discussed in chapter eight).

James 2:13 demonstrates clearly what happens when one succumbs to critical judgment. "For judgment will be merciless to one who has shown no mercy; mercy triumphs over judgment" (NASB).

A merciful person is one who desires the highest and best for all people. Instead of judging various people, a merciful person shows mercy. Even if a person has committed wrongs against him, a merciful person forgives in Jesus' name.

The Lord Jesus expands on this principle in the classic parable on forgiveness found in Matthew 18:23-35. In speaking to the unforgiving servant, Jesus says the lord of the slave declared, " 'Should you not also have had mercy on your fellow-slave, even as I had mercy on you?' And his lord, moved with anger, handed him over to the torturers until he should repay all that was owed him" (vv. 33-34). To which Jesus added: "So shall My heavenly Father also do to you, if each of you does not forgive his brother from your heart" (v. 35) (NASB).

I have seen this principle operate many times. The power of God would not move in a person's life until he had expressed mercy towards someone who had injured him. The offending person doesn't have to express any repentance to the offended individual. All the offended person must do is forgive that other person—even as God for Christ's sake has forgiven him.

When that simple act occurs, it brings power and release into a person's life. Sometimes physical healings occur. Other times unanswered prayers are finally heard. Broken relationships are often restored. In short, God moves!

In the supreme act of forgiveness Jesus, as He hung on the cross, said, "Father forgive them; for they do not know what they are doing" (Luke 23:34 NASB). That same attitude of forgiveness was in Stephen as he was being martyred. "He cried out with a loud voice, 'Lord, do not hold this sin against them!' " (Acts 7:60 NASB).

"Blessed are the pure in heart"

"Blessed are the pure in heart: for they shall see God," says Matthew 5:8.

Being pure in heart is not holiness. The word "holy" (*hagios*) is a different word from the word "pure" (*katharos*). The word "holy" means that something is free of contamination, while being pure in heart means that which is not mixed with anything else.

People who are pure in heart are ones whose lives are not mixed up in other things. They have a heart inclined toward God. They have a singleness of vision. They're not double-minded. By the time a disciple arrives at this point in the Christian life, he knows that Jesus Christ himself is the beginning and end of all that life is about.

The Lord vividly demonstrated this principle to me several years ago. As a Southern Baptist pastor with 20 years' experience in the ministry and degrees from two Southern Baptist schools, I had to make a choice.

In the middle of the tense situation over the baptism with the Holy Spirit, I could have stated, "I believe I'm mistaken. I don't really believe the gift of tongues is for today. I further don't believe I should pray for people to be healed of sicknesses or diseases, and I won't cast out demons in the name of Jesus any longer."

If I had taken that step, I would still have a comfortable retirement program today. I would still live in a handsome pastoral home on the coast of Georgia. I would still be recognized as a leading minister in my town.

Instead, the Lord opened my eyes and I saw something crucial to my Christian experience: I could not deny anything He had done for me. As a result of that choice, my family and I have tested the faithfulness of God. We found He stands behind His promises one hundred percent.

I had loved Jesus practically all my life. When I was twelve years old, I had been born again with supreme confidence I was a child of God. But until I committed myself to a single-hearted devotion to Him, my Christian experience lacked something. Being pure in heart caused me to see God as I had never seen Him before.

Of course, I don't mean I saw God with my physical

eyes. I saw God through His loving handiwork—healing of the sick, demonic bondages broken, families restored. One elderly man was raised off his death bed and was on vacation in Florida the next week. My personal ministry has extended itself far beyond anything I had ever dreamed.

I frequently encounter all kinds of Christians who seem depressed and discouraged. They come from all walks—fundamental, conservative, liberal, orthodox, full gospel. At one time, they were excited about Jesus. But now, cares of the world have crept in.

Little resentments and old bitternesses have returned. They've relaxed in their prayer and Bible study. Some no longer pray in the Spirit daily. In brief, they've lost that single-hearted devotion to Jesus. They are no longer able to "see God."

All these disciples need to do is allow Jesus Christ to become first in every decision of life. When a believer is pure in heart, he can see God in the midst of adverse circumstance. No force can overcome a disciple whose eyes are on Jesus. That's exactly who Stephen saw (Acts 7:56).

"Blessed are the peacemakers"

Matthew 5:9 says, "Blessed are the peacemakers: for they shall be called the children of God."

The Lord Jesus came to earth as a peacemaker. On the night of His birth, the angels announced His arrival with a proclamation of peace and good will toward "all men." Jesus came to bring peace between God and fallen man.

Jesus made it clear that His disciples would be peacemakers. They were expected to take the gift of peace which Jesus personally delivered (John 14:27) and pass it to others. The peacemaker's work would result in the restoration of God's blessings to His people.

The Greek word for peace is *eirenē*. It is similar to the Hebrew word *shalom* in a number of ways. The blessing within shalom contains every possible benefit man can receive from God—health, prosperity, wholesome relationships with others and restoration of spiritual union with God. This mighty resource has been given to the disciple of Jesus Christ so that he might pass it to others.

Jesus expected His disciples to work establishing peace between their neighbors and God. The disciple does this by introducing Jesus as the "gift" of God's love. That is the goal of every mature disciple—bringing his neighbor to Jesus, who then escorts him into the Father's presence.

We have two sons who are "live wires" in many respects. At times, conflicts arise because of their differing interests and unlimited energies. When that happens, dad or mom has to engage in peacemaking. After determining the disagreement's cause, we correct, discipline and finally require they forgive each other. When forgiveness occurs, their attitudes change and peace is restored.

A disciple who matures to the place of becoming a peacemaker is also called a "son of God." The King James Version translates the text "children" in verse nine, while the New American Standard Bible translates it "sons of God."

The Greek word used in the text is *huios*, which means son, instead of the word *teknos*, which means child. There is a significant difference in being a child or a son. A disciple's relationship with God begins at a childlike level. However, the Father's greater purpose is for that relationship to mature to sonship or partnership with Him. The latter is a truly responsible position in the kingdom of God. The concept of sonship as partnership with God is discussed in greater detail in chapter nine.

After the disciple matures to the place of being a peacemaker, Jesus showed, he will be as helpless as he was at the start. When he becomes mature enough to handle "persecution for righteousness' sake," God will be his only defense. The disciple will never lose this basic dependence upon God. It is an essential element of his discipleship.

7 | *The Disciple's Role in the World*

Without question, every Christian struggles with his role in the world. How should a believer conduct himself—mild-mannered and marshmellowy, or bold and aggressive?

The answer produces a wide variety of responses on the part of God's people. Some attempt to boldly "force-feed" the gospel upon the unsaved. Others resort to "secret sainthood," claiming they believe while ignoring the need for fellowship in the Christian community. Many become frustrated at how to function and quit altogether.

Anyone whose life has been genuinely changed by Christ should want to express the good news. But how? Must we all employ bright lapel buttons proclaiming the news? Or stand on street corners passing out gospel tracts?

How can a disciple function in the world as Jesus intended?

Immediately after introducing the Beatitudes to His

disciples, Jesus answered that very question in the next four verses.

He said: "You are the salt of the earth; but if the salt has become tasteless, how will it be made salty again? It is good for nothing any more, except to be thrown out and trampled under foot by men" (Matt. 5:13 NASB).

It is precisely because a disciple sees himself—by faith—as salt that he can actively penetrate the world for Jesus Christ. Many people feel inadequate in sharing their witness for Christ. Some actually believe they're not qualified to explain their Christian experience to a nonbeliever.

Yet Jesus took none of these notions into consideration. He simply called His disciples to accept their roles in the world—by faith!

Theologian Elton Trueblood says in *The Yoke of Christ*, "The statement of Christ which follows immediately after the Beatitudes is really amazing. What Jesus says is that there is a special way in which the world can be kept from decay and that the world is to be saved by a particular kind of penetration. In the days of Christ the only way to preserve meat was by the use of salt. By this practice, then as now, meat could be kept a long time."[1]

When I was a young boy growing up in rural Alabama, my father slaughtered farm animals during the wintertime. When November came bringing a chill with it, everybody knew it was time to kill our hogs which had been fattening all year long.

The meat was placed into large containers and completely immersed in salt. The salt would then begin the preserving process.

At times during the preserving, the salt absorbed the

[1]Elton Trueblood, *The Yoke of Christ*, (Waco, Texas: Word Books, 1958) p. 28

meat's flavor. It also frequently got mixed with debris in the container. When that happened, the salt had to be thrown out after the meat was removed. It was no longer pure salt. It had, as Jesus observed, "lost its savour and become tasteless."

Kenneth Scott Latourette in *A History of Christianity* points out there was a tendency for disciples to withdraw from the world in the early stages of the monastic movement instead of seeking to save it.[2] That tendency is still around. People have moved into communities, attempting to preserve the quality of Christian life but also isolating themselves from the world.

If all believers moved into cloistered relationships in communities, who would be left to be the "salt" of the world?

Because Christians have the redemptive power of God working within them, they should learn to function in the world, while they maintain a freedom from the world's influence.

Without the presence of Christians, the world would have decayed more rapidly than it has. The disciple brings a preserving influence to a chaotic world. He must therefore see himself as an essential part of his community.

The Bible says that David saw his day. He realized its arrival. He knew the direction of his life's mission. His presence was a preserving influence in the world.

This sense of mission was also in Jesus Christ. He came into the world with one purpose—to do the will of the Father. Because He kept that purpose continually before Him, Jesus succeeded in fulfilling His mission. In the same way, Jesus indicated this sense of mission should be

[2]Kenneth Scott Latourette, *A History of Christianity*, (New York: Harper & Row, 1953) p. 222

part of each disciple's outlook.

When a disciple understands he is the "salt of the earth," his life takes on new meaning. He gains a fresh sense of destiny, mission and purpose. His every waking moment provides fresh opportunities to fulfill this special mission.

Elton Trueblood writes: "The Company of Jesus is not people streaming to a shrine; and it is not people making up an audience for a speaker; it is laborers engaged in the harvesting task of reaching their perplexed and seeking brethren with something so vital that, if it is received, it will change their lives."[3]

Salt as a Purifier and Flavor

Salt not only preserves but it purifies. The mineral actually possesses healing qualities. Thus the presence of a Christian in a community is that of a purifying agent. By his very presence, a Christian announces to the world that God has broken into human affairs through the person of Jesus Christ.

As salt is used by an expert cook to flavor food, the heavenly Father flavors the earth by the presence of Christians. The world's unredeemed element actually enjoys the blessings that come because of the believers' presence. Without that, the world would be a totally distasteful place in which to live.

So the disciple must see himself, not only as a preserving and purifying influence in the world, but also a flavoring quality. This attribute gives a sense of self-confidence to the believer. He understands his presence releases the love and power of God to others. How else could God demonstrate these qualities?

[3]Elton Trueblood, *The Company of the Committed*, (New York: Harper & Row, 1961) p. 45

When a disciple learns to be comfortable in his role, he will have what I call "coffee cup Christianity." He will be able to function anywhere in the world and comfortably give his witness for Jesus Christ. He can sit down in a diner or an elegant restaurant—just over a simple cup of coffee—and share his witness with others.

Jesus vividly demonstrated this principle throughout His earthly life. He was just as comfortable with a group of publicans and sinners as He was with the most devout followers. Jesus could do this because He understood His mission. He realized His purpose in life. Equally as much, He wanted His disciples to understand this dynamic principle of the Christian life.

Salt Can Lose its Savor

If I permit my attitude to be altered by the world's pressure, I will soon lose my preserving, purifying, flavoring influence. My attitude will have been mixed with the customs and attitudes on the earth. I will have lost the mission I was called to fulfill.

When a believer arrives at that condition, just like salt, Jesus said, he "is good for nothing any more, except to be thrown out and trampled under foot by men."

This condition can occur in a disciple's life. He can lose a sense of mission and direction. In time he can even lose his effective witness for the Lord. He has lost his saltiness or savor.

Says Trueblood from *The Yoke of Christ*, "Jesus recognized that although the only way to preserve the world by this particular kind of salt, there was also a way in which it could be lost. At first it is difficult for us to understand Christ's reference to the loss of saltness, because we know from our chemical studies that pure salt is always salt. It does not lose its saltness. Pure sodium chloride does not deteriorate. What then did He mean?

"The salt with which Christ was familiar was a crude composite such as would be familiar on the shores of the Dead Sea or the Mediterranean Sea. This salt could be so adulterated as to be essentially lost. A great deal of it would not be salt at all, but other crude material, and it would stand in piles, not so different from those which we can see today on the shores of San Francisco Bay, where the salt is heaped up before it is refined.

"As these piles would stand out in the open in the rain, frequently the salt would be washed out and nothing would remain but the dross, with no true saltness left. The point of Christ's words is that the residue is absolutely worthless. It is not worth a little; it is worth nothing!"[4]

When salt is mixed with other chemicals, it loses its potency and power. The same is true for the "salt of the earth." When disciples of Jesus Christ get mixed up in the things of the world, they lose their effectiveness.

Jesus spoke to this condition when He said, "Blessed are the pure in heart." Even while walking this earthly plane, these are disciples who have a single-hearted devotion to God.

The Disciple as Light

"You are the light of the world. A city set on a hill cannot be hidden. Nor do men light a lamp, and put it under the peckmeasure, but on the lampstand; and it gives light to all who are in the house. Let your light shine before men in such a way that they may see your good

[4]Trueblood, op. cit., p. 28

works, and glorify your Father who is in heaven" (Matt. 5:14-16 NASB).

Jesus said His disciples *are* the light of the world. Just as the case with being the "salt of the earth," he wanted them to see they are the light of the world—right now!

As soon as a disciple has been recruited into the army of the King, he is expected to see himself as the light of the world. Thus he becomes willing to let that light shine through his life.

Being the light of the world and bearing witness in the world are two of the most difficult aspects of the Christian life. Listen to the observations of Elton Trueblood from *The Yoke of Christ* in this regard:

"It is curious to see how we are more afraid of being sanctimonious than of being wicked. Many would hate worse to be called a saint than to be called a sinner. We never boast of our virtue, but we are extremely prone to boast of our vice. Some of those, particularly students, who were questioned in connection with the preparation of the Kinsey Reports on contemporary sex life, came out of the interviews telling how they boasted of sins which they had never committed.

"In many circles this is the only way in which young people can save face at all. But, of course, this is far from new. In his *Confessions* written more than fifteen hundred years ago, Augustine of Hippo told with keen psychological insight how he had been 'ashamed to be shameless.' "[5]

I know exactly what Trueblood means. While I was attending a Baptist college in Tennessee, I met a young man who continually bragged about his manly exploits. Many other students, as well as myself, recognized he was

[5]Ibid., p. 100

describing experiences that never happened. It was almost as if he were trying to establish credibility with us through these fantasized tales.

Often, in testifying of his conversion, it is easier for a person to talk about his sinful background than the goodness of God working in his life. Many testimonies are three-fourths about the person's past—at times in detail or in a bragging fashion—and one-fourth about the redemptive work of Jesus Christ.

Some months ago our fellowship in Brunswick had an outside speaker. The young man spent so much time dwelling on this past life of sin he had to be encouraged to move on to glorifying Jesus Christ. Congregations can often vicariously enjoy the old sins described in a person's testimony. Unfortunately, such testimonies are out of focus.

In order to see yourself as the light of the world, a disciple must move beyond the sinful past and into the glorious present with Christ. In examining the second chapter of Acts, it is evident the newly converted believers spent little time in talking about their old sins. Thus they were freed to let their light shine. They did it boldly and without fear—rapidly spreading the faith in the process.

The average person who calls himself a Christian does not want to bear witness in the world. For sure, it is not easy. Many believers feel uncomfortable and nervous about witnessing. I have seen this happen even in the safe confines of the church. As a pastor, I knew not to call upon some people to pray out loud. They would be simply too embarrassed to handle the task. They had never settled the issue in their hearts that they are already the light of the world.

Bearing witness (or letting your light shine) is the basic thrust of the Christian community. It is the foundation upon which the Christian church is built, as each disciple sees he is a witness. As that light shines out or as that witness is given, new recruits are brought into the family of God. Without it, the church dies out.

From *The Yoke of Christ*, Elton Trueblood says, "There is amazing power in the life of an individual or a church or a people, in which there is a willingness to make a witness, regardless of what people say. So long as we have our ears open for the remarks of others, much of our strength is dissipated. The way of power is that according to which we have our eyes on the task rather than on what people may think or say. If we are trying to be popular, we shall often be miserable, for human responses are notoriously fickle. The Christian answer is, 'They say, let them say!' Our responsibility is not to win approval, but to be faithful. A faith about which we are apologetic is practically worthless. . . ."[6]

The case for bearing witness was never more strongly made than when Jesus stood before Pilate. "For this I have been born, and for this I have come into the world, to bear witness to the truth," Jesus declared (John 18:37 NASB).

The Lord Jesus came witnessing of God's redemptive plan for all mankind. That was His role. A disciple's role is to bear witness of Jesus. That is accomplished by letting your light shine.

Of course, no man can make another man a witness for Christ. Being a witness is a divine act of God's grace. When Jesus called His disciples, He was actually enlisting

[6]Ibid., pp. 106-107

a company of witnesses. Many false cults have captured this truth, producing scores of followers for their movements. At the other extreme, the Christian church has failed in some cases to understand its role as a company of witnesses.

In calling the disciples, the command was to "follow" Jesus. As that command was obeyed, the disciples became "fishers of men." The same is true today. As men and women follow Jesus Christ, they become the light of the world, drawing attention to Him as the Savior of mankind. In turn, this causes others to see their need for Jesus. They repent and turn to Him. And that is what the gospel is all about.

The end result of the disciple's efforts, Jesus showed, was that people would "glorify your Father which is in heaven." People would not get the credit. God would.

<h1>8 | Forces That Hinder Discipleship</h1>

Jesus expected His disciples to oversee the emerging church in a mature way after He was gone. His followers could not accomplish that job unless they understood the way the enemy works to weaken both the disciple and the church. "Behold I send you out as sheep in the midst of wolves," Jesus instructed them. "Therefore, be shrewd as serpents and innocent as doves" (Matt. 10:16 NASB).

The battle between the Church and the powers of darkness grows more intense as the disciple matures. At the peak of his maturity, he can expect persecution (Matt. 5:10-12). He must recognize what is happening so he won't be slain in the heat of battle by the "arrows of the wicked one" (Eph. 6:16).

After introducing His disciples to the Beatitudes and their role in the world, Jesus explained six danger points which each disciple must contend with personally. He also instructed them on the debilitating power of tradition. The scribes and Pharisees had already fallen into its snare. The disciples of Christ were expected to avoid it.

The Restraint of Tradition

Mama shouted that day in 1955 when I was ordained in the little Baptist church in Tennessee. When the meeting dismissed, I was embarrassed and walked quickly back to her seat. I had never heard her shout before in church.

"I just couldn't contain myself," she explained, her eyes wet with tears. "I prayed for a boy before you were born and I dedicated you to God's service at birth." She had kept the secret in her heart, telling no one. Now all her dreams were realized. Her boy had become a Baptist preacher.

And for the next eighteen years, that was my calling in life—being a Baptist preacher pastoring large, successful Southern Baptist churches. But in 1973 I was no longer "just" a Baptist preacher. I had experienced a personal "pentecost" similar to that in the Acts of the Apostles and I was on a direct collision course with my Baptist tradition.

Instead of going to the Holy Scriptures to test my experience, church leaders, who challenged me, used the 1929 Southern Baptist Statement of Faith to prove my heresy. Although Baptist leaders have always considered the Holy Bible "as the true center for Christian union and the supreme standard by which all human conduct, creeds and opinions should be tried," it was not used to challenge me.

I was caught in my own tradition!

The Bible allowed a baptism in the Holy Spirit, encouraged it and gave directions on how to receive it. Yet, my tradition said it couldn't be.

Tradition is usually established in the church when the first generation passes off the scene and a new generation assumes control. Most Christian movements began through the personal experience of a person or a group, leading them to band together for worship and mutual encouragement.

Growth in the movement required greater organization and statements or confessions of faith which, in effect, were like the code or oral tradition of the scribes and Pharisees. Subsequent generations sought to follow the confessions of faith instead of the living God. Their protection of father's confessions became a "tradition" to believe instead of the Word of God to obey.

When that condition happens, tradition has replaced the authority of the Holy Scriptures. Any interpretation or code will naturally become the guide for faith and practice for the Christian committed to his church's doctrine but ignorant of the Word of God.

"Do not think that I came to abolish the Law or the Prophets; I did not come to abolish, but to fulfill. For truly I say to you, until heaven and earth pass away, not the smallest letter or stroke shall pass away from the Law, until all is accomplished.

"Whoever then annuls one of the least of these commandments, and so teaches others, shall be called least in the kingdom of heaven; but whoever keeps and teaches them, he shall be called great in the kingdom of heaven.

"For I say to you, that unless your righteousness surpasses that of the scribes and Pharisees, you shall not enter the kingdom of heaven" (Matt. 5:17-20 NASB).

When the Scripture refers to the Law or the Prophets,

it could be referring to four different possibilities—the Ten Commandments; the Pentateuch, which is the first five books of the Bible attributed to Moses; the Old Covenant or the Old Testament; and, last, the oral or scribal law.

In the time of Jesus, it was the fourth meaning—oral or scribal law—which was most commonly accepted as the Law. It was, of course, this scribal law which Jesus and the apostle Paul condemned.

The Old Testament has broad principles which man must take and apply to his life under God's guidance. The later Jews argued that this was not enough. They argued that rules needed to be established so that all men could consistently obey the rules which they alone decided were genuine Old Testament principles.

Out of this came a disciplined order of men called the scribes who devoted their lives to putting the Old Testament principles into hundreds of rules and regulations. These rules and regulations were then transmitted verbally from one generation to another. This became the oral or scribal law.

For instance, the scribes recalled, "God said to remember the sabbath day and to keep it holy, six days you shall work and the seventh day you shall rest." The scribes decided it was too difficult for the common people to understand what is work and what isn't. Thus they interpreted the Old Testament law.

This is why Jesus ran into conflict with the Pharisees when His disciples took some grain from the wheat field on the sabbath (Matt. 12:1-8). Small amounts of the wheat were supposedly left for the poor and the hungry. But the Pharisees reacted strongly when the disciples gathered grain. "If you harvest any grain on the sabbath, you're working," they charged.

Jesus faced the same problem for healing on the sabbath. " 'Is it lawful to heal on the sabbath days?' they asked him, that they might accuse him" (verse 10).

Responding to such legalism, Jesus said, "What man shall there be among you, who shall have one sheep, and if it falls into a pit on the Sabbath, will he not take hold of it, and lift it out? Of how much more value then is a man than a sheep! So then, it is lawful to do good on the Sabbath" (Matt. 12:11-12 NASB).

The Psalmist David wrote, "The law of the Lord is perfect, restoring the soul . . ." (Ps. 19:7 NASB). As a believer comes to understand the heavenly Father's great provision, he recognizes the law is a pearl of great price—a precious gift. It becomes a roadmap through this earthly life, not a burden. It only becomes a burden when someone tries to legalistically expand on the message of God.

That is exactly what the scribes did. Attempting to help people understand the Old Testament laws, they complicated the picture with a complex set of rules and regulations. Eventually—around the middle of the third century A.D.—the oral law was written down into a code. It was called the Mishnah.

But that was not enough. Scholars came behind that work saying, "The code needs interpreting." They wrote a commentary of the Mishnah so that the common people could understand the code of the law. Ultimately these scholars produced twelve volumes of material called the Talmud.

This situation reminds me of the complex rules and

regulations of the Internal Revenue Service. Most laymen cannot read an IRS code book. It's necessary to get a representative who can explain, not the law, but the code of the law.

Not only did Jesus have to contend with the scribes and their mindboggling interpretations of the law, but He also faced another militant group known as the Pharisees. Pharisee means "separated one." They were an order of men who separated themselves from ordinary society to devote their lives to keeping the rules and regulations of the scribes. They publicly demonstrated these rules of conduct for the lesser devout Jews. This placed the Pharisees out on the street—praying, giving alms, and, in particular, calling attention to themselves.

In the time of Christ, the Pharisees had already existed for some two hundred years and were a strongly established, powerful religious-political party. One can imagine the dilemma of the average Jew trying to live up to these hundreds of scribal rules, and then watching the pious and meaningless exercises of the Pharisees in public. The Jew simply could not break through to a loving and compassionate God.

Tradition will do that to you. It will literally freeze you out of the presence of God.

If most people are honest, they can see much of their behavior as a Christian is governed by tradition instead of the Word of God. As a Southern Baptist pastor, I was deeply committed to my tradition. Yet being committed to that tradition produced a giant conflict in me. I struggled many times between that tradition and the Word of God. I saw myself frequently trying to protect that tradition even though it was producing a void in me.

Finally, in His great mercy, God broke into my life through the power of the Holy Spirit. He made it clear all I needed to do was get into the presence of Jesus. If I could reach Jesus, He would literally fulfill all that my tradition spoke towards.

Through these Scriptures, Jesus gave His disciples important insight into walking with Him. The insight was simple—the moment a disciple comes under the law of tradition, he is bound. Every follower of Jesus must live above that. Every disciple's first love must be the Lord Jesus Christ.

"I want you to know," Jesus said in essence, "not a single stroke in any letter of the Hebrew or Aramaic languages will be removed in any way from what God has said. But I did not come to do away with these Laws, I came to fulfill—for in My Person, I am the fulfillment of everything God has said."

Six Danger Areas

After drawing attention to himself (Matt. 5:17-20) as the fulfillment of God's Word, Jesus drew a further distinction between the ancients' teachings and His own meaning. In Matthew 5:21-48, He interpreted these distinctions through six behavioral traits to be developed in the disciple's life. These behavioral traits or danger areas can be used to disrupt a Christian's walk in the Spirit quicker than anything else. They work like binding cords, restraining the believer from achieving his maximum potential in the Lord.

The teachings of Jesus were very practical for the discerning disciple. There was nothing secretive or complicated about what He said. The Lord told His followers how to get to the roots of their problems. He knew that maturity came in dealing with the *roots*, not the *results* of sin. Dealing with the results is punishment. Dealing with the roots is discipleship. Disciples of Jesus will learn the difference.

The Restraint of Anger

Anger is the number one killer of love, joy and peace within the body of Christ. As a pastor with years of counseling experience, I have observed that more people slip in their relationship to God and more homes are disrupted over anger than any other cause.

Jesus introduced this problem because He knew His disciples would be continually wrestling with it. That was evident during the Lord's earthly ministry, when crowds mobbed Him and disputes broke out even among the disciples. Those problems intensified after the Holy Spirit came and three thousand were won to Christ in a single day. It was only natural that problems would arise in dealing with people. After all, it was the problems of life that drew people like a magnet to Jesus and His disciples.

It may seem surprising that problems and wrong attitudes surfaced between the disciples before Jesus ascended—but, in fact, the Scriptures record they *happened*. Some of the disciples were exasperated with the multitudes, wanting to send them away before Jesus had a chance to perform a miracle. Then one day the mother of two disciples came to Jesus with her sons in tow. She had a request to make.

"Grant that these my two sons may sit, the one on thy right hand, and the other on the left, in thy kingdom," she asked (Matt. 20:21). Verse 24 then makes an interesting observation: "And hearing this, the ten became indignant at the two brothers" (NASB). They were angry.

Knowing that anger would be a constant problem, Jesus dealt with it first. "Ye have heard that it was said by them of old time, Thou shalt not kill; and whosoever shall kill shall be in danger of the judgment" (Matt.5:21).

The contrast is apparent in the verse. The ancients were told about murder from one generation to another by oral transmission. "But I say unto you," he proclaimed in verse 22, "That whosoever is angry with his brother without a cause shall be in danger of the judgment: and whosoever shall say to his brother, Raca, shall be in danger of the council: but whosoever shall say, Thou fool, shall be in danger of hell fire."

In focusing on anger, Jesus never said a believer couldn't express disagreement with another. On the contrary, He unquestionably called disciples to express themselves to others and then jointly seek the will of God.

There are two words in the Greek that express anger. One word (*thumos*) describes the kind that rises quickly but subsides just as fast—like the anger of a small child. Most everyone has seen that kind of anger. Two small boys are out playing in the yard. Something happens and all at once they're fighting. But shortly they resolve the problem and they're back playing. All is forgiven and forgotten.

There is nothing destructive about that kind of anger. In fact, that kind can be constructive and helpful. It can stimulate dialogue between two people. My wife and I have learned this sort of anger can be beneficial in the home.

But the type of anger Jesus describes here is not the type which vanishes easily. The word in the text is *orgizesthai*. It is a long-lasting, brooding anger. It can be so heavy in home situations that family members just can't work out problems. It is a disruptive force. At times, it opens doors allowing people to reach into the skeleton closet and bring back long-forgotten situations. Jesus said if a disciple entertains this kind of anger he will be judged for it.

According to Jesus, the act of murder has its roots in anger. A housewife came to my office one day confirming that fact. Her Baptist preacher husband was away from home most of the time. She was left with small children and the total responsibility of running the house. For months, she had no free time for herself. Her deep, brooding anger had burst into near tragedy that morning.

As one of her crying children tugged at her skirt for attention, she suddenly found herself in a wild rage—a sharp kitchen knife in her hand. Her brooding anger had expressed itself in a gesture of murder. She had deep guilt in her heart to think she would do such a thing. After she released her angry feelings toward her husband and children, she was freed from this binding force.

The word "raca" is hard to translate because it is more of an attitude, a tone of voice or a contemptible response than anything else. It's as if someone reacted to a person's actions by saying, "You empty-headed idiot. You good-for-nothing person. I didn't expect any more of you." Such action will get you into trouble with your society, Jesus indicated.

Finally, the one who says "thou fool" (*moros*), demonstrates a contempt and disrespect for the moral character of another human being—a life that God cares for. That person would be "guilty enough to go into the hell of fire," Jesus said.

The "hell of fire" mentioned in verse 22 is a place called Gehenna or the Valley of Hinnom which is located south and west of Jerusalem. It separates Mount Zion to the north and the plain of Rephaim to the south.

Ahaz and Manasseh made their children "pass through the fire" in this valley (2 Kings 16:3; 2 Chron. 28:3, 33:6), and the custom of infant sacrifice to the fire gods was also practiced there. Because of this, Josiah cursed the place (2 Kings 23:10, 13-14; 2 Chron. 34:4-5). Thus it became the common cesspool of the city into which its sewage was conducted by the waters of the Kidron and where all its solid filth was collected and burned. The later Jews applied the name Gehenna to denote the place of eternal torment.

From the garbage pits of this valley came a worm that was practically impossible to destroy. Isaiah 66:24 is one of several places in Scripture that refers to a "worm shall not die, neither shall their fire be quenched."

The destructive power of such anger will eat away the inner peace of a disciple, leaving him a disrupted, anxious individual. Only God can restore what the cankerworm has eaten.

The Restraint of Lust

"Ye have heard that it was said by them of old time, Thou shalt not commit adultery: But I say unto you, That whosoever looketh on a woman to lust after her hath committed adultery with her already in his heart" (Matt. 5:27-28).

The concept of lusting after another person is that of

desiring someone to the extent of fantasizing what it would be like to complete a sexual encounter with that person. James gave a picture of how lust works: "When lust has conceived, it gives birth to sin; and when sin is accomplished, it brings forth death" (James 1:15 NASB).

Each disciple needs to step into a mature understanding of his sexuality. Not only is this true in general relationships with the opposite sex, but also with husbands, wives, sons and daughters. Many seem bound by fears that prevent them from settling into a normal, healthy understanding of themselves.

Jesus was saying to His disciples, "Live in the world of reality." That means learn your role in life and be comfortable with it. There is much confusion throughout society today because people are controlled by emotional whims and not the Word of God. The Bible speaks plainly that there are relationships God blesses and there are others which are sinful.

After focusing on this problem, Jesus gave some practical advice in verses 29 and 30. "And if your right eye makes you stumble, tear it out, and throw it from you; for it is better for you that one of the parts of your body perish, than for your whole body to be thrown into hell. And if your right hand makes you stumble, cut it off, and throw it from you; for it is better for you that one of the parts of your body perish, than for your whole body to go into hell" (NASB).

Obviously, Jesus was not approaching this problem in an actual physical sense. However, man does have the power within himself to say, "Eye, in the name of Jesus, I command you to be single." If a disciple's eye causes him to stumble, Jesus expects that follower to deal with it.

The enemy knows that lust begins in the eye. That's why the world is saturated with pictures, both printed and audio-visual. Pictures encourage men and women to lust. Hundreds of products—from cars and clothes to toothpaste—are sold through eye appeal, much of it sexually oriented.

So Jesus said, "If you cut lust off at the eye, you will have the problem solved. But if you don't stop it at the eye, it will move from the eye to the hand."

My wife and I recognized this when our sons began to walk. As they began taking their first steps around the house, if they ever saw an interesting object, they next wanted to touch it. Many adults are the same way today. The prince of darkness knows this. Thus he constantly introduces eye-appealing objects. If the disciple doesn't deal with it properly, the next step involves touching.

Men and women who work together in the closed quarters of an office don't understand this principle. Sometimes nothing more than a quick glance or a casual touch will arouse deep lustful emotions. The result can be sin.

The Lord gave a simple approach in dealing with lust. In fact, the approach is so simple, many can't accept it. When confronted with lust, simply look the other way.

I had a missionary friend who was my partner for several years in Spain. He frequently prayed a short prayer I have never forgotten. "Lord, keep my eye single and always fixed on Jesus." They are words well worth remembering and following.

The Restraint of Disrespect

"It hath been said, Whosoever shall put away his wife,

let him give her a writing of divorcement: But I say unto you, That whosoever shall put away his wife, saving for the cause of fornication, causeth her to commit adultery: and whosoever shall marry her that is divorced committeth adultery" (Matt. 5:31-32).

The time in which Jesus lived had witnessed some amazing interpretations of the law. Men had been given complete liberty to keep their wives in bondage. With the aid of a certificate of divorcement, a husband would dismiss his wife for any minor reason.

The situation had reached the point a man could get up one morning, look at his wife and say, "You no longer please me. Therefore, I have a right to divorce you." He could then walk to the city square, make a verbal declaration and free himself. The wife was then forced out of the house. In many cases, women had to resort to begging or prostitution to survive.

The church has experienced wide-ranging teaching on the roles of women and wives and how they should function in the body of Christ. Unfortunately, much teaching has relegated them to subhuman levels. "Submission" was the only word heard in some teaching.

Jesus Christ was a revolutionary in women's rights. He respected women and elevated the dignity of all women.

Joel 2:28 made it clear during the outpouring of the Holy Spirit that sons and *daughters* shall prophesy. Some people have given Paul credit for silencing women in the church but the apostle acknowledged (1 Cor. 11:5) that the Holy Spirit moves upon women in prayer and prophecy. Not only that, but Paul says the woman is the glory of the man (1 Cor. 11:7).

The Scripture declares there is neither male or female. In Christ Jesus, they are equal. Within the home, of course, there are distinctive roles. The head of every woman is the man. The head of the man is Christ. This order gives balance to the home. It also produces liberty in relationships, not bondage.

Many women—especially those in the feminist movement—say they are second-class citizens unless they are given equality of opportunity. Satan has disrupted society to the point many don't understand the biblical role they should be fulfilling. Hence, much trouble results.

Numerous Bible teachers and preachers have viewed Matthew 5:31-32 only in the context of divorce. However, I am convinced Jesus was calling His disciples to look at a far broader subject—appreciation and respect for womanhood. The Lord was showing His disciples they would become more effective ambassadors of the gospel if they properly respected and treated women. Peter obviously learned well, for later he states the man who does not live with his wife in an "understanding way" will find his prayers hindered (1 Peter 3:7 NASB).

A man who had been hurt by women many times in life went to a monastery one day and offered himself as a monk. When the abbot interviewed him, the man said candidly, "I've been hurt again and again. I can't stand people anymore—particularly women. I've come here to be a monk for the rest of my days. I want to devote myself to the Lord totally."

"I'm sorry," the wise abbot responded. "We can't use you here."

The man was puzzled. "But I don't understand," he

said. "I thought you were in need of people to carry on the Lord's work here."

"Oh, we are," the abbot answered softly, "but you're not ready for this place. You need to go back out into the world and ask God to restore a respect for womanhood in you. If you can reach the point of forgiving those who have hurt you and even progress to the point you want a wife but are willing to give it all up for Jesus, then come. You will make a good monk then."

The same is true today. The doorway to effective discipleship in many cases is through a proper appreciation and respect for God's creation—woman.

The Restraint of Unreliability

"Again, ye have heard that it hath been said by them of old time, Thou shalt not forswear thyself, but shalt perform unto the Lord thine oaths: But I say unto you, Swear not at all; neither by heaven; for it is God's throne: Nor by the earth; for it is his footstool: neither by Jerusalem; for it is the city of the great King.

"Neither shalt thou swear by thy head, because thou canst not make one hair white or black. But let your communication be, Yea, yea; Nay, nay: for whatsoever is more than these cometh of evil" (Matt. 5:33-37).

In the time of Jesus, the average Jew had reached the point in his religious experience that when he made an oath it was easy to discern whether or not the man was telling the truth. It is not much different today even in Christian circles. Have you ever noticed that quality about people?

The pastor is often expected to visit people in their homes in the South. During these visits, people almost always promise to come to church on Sunday. Yet by their very choice of words, I have learned they won't be there when Sunday arrives.

"Ya'll come to see us sometime" is a frequently heard expression in the South. However, it's not a genuine invitation to visit. It's simply a polite expression. Don't visit people who say it, because they aren't actually expecting you.

If a disciple of Christ has to be pinned down under oath to tell the truth, something is wrong with the foundation of his faith. Speaking the truth should be basic to every follower of Jesus Christ. Paul admonished believers to speak the truth "in love" (Eph. 4:15). Jesus called His followers to say "yes" when that was the correct answer and to say "no" when that was correct. Out of politeness, some people simply won't say "no."

My father used to say, "Let your word be your bond." In his day, a written contract wasn't necessary if a man gave another person "his word." Today, a person needs an airtight contract drafted by a Philadelphia lawyer to get some people—even Christians—to simply keep their word.

The Scriptures exhort Christians to be totally honest in an incredibly dishonest world. If a disciple makes a promise, he should keep it. If a follower of Jesus has legitimate financial obligations, he should pay them. In simplest form, this is discipleship: the Jesus view.

In counseling people with financial problems, I've found they buy items on credit—often over and beyond their means to pay. A crisis occurs and they can't meet the obligation. Instead of calling the store where the debit is owed, these Christians blindly ignore the matter. In many cases, that's all they have to do. Yet the problem is often compounded by refusing to make a simple telephone call.

The Lord convicted me similarly of making promises to my children and not keeping them. At times, I'd promise to take them fishing or play baseball. If something else came up, though, I'd break my promise. The same has been true with my wife. I'd sacrifice time with her for some other pressing matter, even after I had made a clear-cut promise. If the faith of Christian fathers is to be real, it must be acted out before children—and mothers.

The Restraint of Retaliation

"Ye have heard that it hath been said, An eye for an eye, and a tooth for a tooth: But I say unto you, That ye resist not evil: but whosoever shall smite thee on thy right cheek, turn to him the other also. And if any man will sue thee at the law, and take away thy coat, let him have thy cloke also.

"And whosoever shall compel thee to go a mile, go with him twain. Give to him that asketh thee, and from him that would borrow of thee turn not thou away" (Matt. 5:38-42).

Roman law said one who was a native of a territory occupied by the Roman government was required to carry the burden of a Roman soldier for one mile. If a soldier said, "Pick up my pack and carry it," you were required to do exactly that.

Interestingly enough, Jesus came right behind that saying not to walk just one mile, "Go with him two." The disciple may find himself in a situation where he meets demands that appear greater than he can bear. Jesus expected His disciples to mature to the place where they could actually look at an overbearing person as one who needed God's love.

The first mile, Jesus indicated, was a legal requirement. The second mile was an opportunity. The disciple has 5,280 feet, about 1,760 steps for a good-sized man, to witness to the overbearing person about Jesus. The disciple had his attention. During the second mile, the Roman soldier would demand to know why he was walking another mile. No one could ask for a better opportunity to witness. It takes a mature disciple to handle difficult situations in that way.

Retaliation was not in the heart of Jesus. There were many times it could have happened. The scribes and Pharisees were constantly throwing theological brickbats attempting to trip Him. The Lord's purpose and methods were frequently misunderstood by His family and friends. It was strictly Christ's obedience to the Father that brought Him success.

If Jesus had reacted or retaliated at any point along the way, the Father's great redemptive plan for the human race could have been lost. The entire master plan could have been torpedoed. But Jesus kept the faith and God's great plan of love and forgiveness was spread throughout the world. Praise God!

Jesus knew the threat retaliation posed to His disciples. He knew they would be called upon to endure many hardships and trials in proclaiming the gospel. Therefore it was essential that they understood this principle. Retaliation, just like anger, will stifle a disciple's effectiveness for Jesus.

Believers will have the opportunity to proclaim Christ many times by simply turning the other cheek or walking the second mile with a problem-beseiged person. Many

Christians slip and fall when the temptation to retaliate comes. It is in the second mile that God's redemption begins to work. This is especially true among family members who do not understand the life-changing Christian experience. It is also true on the job, where a newly Spirit-baptized believer might be considered "weird."

The Restraint of Jealousy

"Ye have heard that it hath been said, Thou shalt love thy neighbour, and hate thine enemy. But I say unto you, Love your enemies, bless them that curse you, do good to them that hate you, and pray for them which despitefully use you, and persecute you; That ye may be the children of your Father which is in heaven: for he maketh his sun to rise on the evil and on the good, and sendeth rain on the just and on the unjust.

"For if ye love them which love you, what reward have ye? do not even the publicans the same? And if ye salute your brethren only, what do ye more than others? do not even the publicans so? Be ye therefore perfect, even as your Father which is in heaven is perfect" (Matt. 5:43-48).

"Why do the righteous suffer?" is one of the ageless questions in the minds of people since the time of Job. The believer often sees his neighbor cheat on a business partner to gain more wealth. He watches another man charge excessive prices for his product to pay for a home on the lake. Noticing these people acquire wealth while he never seems to "get ahead," the believer resents his neighbor with a deep jealousy.

Did you know the average Christian won't pray for his enemy? He's basically jealous of him. Have you ever heard a Christian say, "I wonder why God blesses that person. He does nothing to serve God. Yet look at all those material things he has. Why doesn't God bless me? I serve Him all the time."

Now you can see the root of the disciple's problem. He doesn't understand his relationship to God. The disciple who can't pray for those who persecute him will have trouble in his relationship to the heavenly Father.

Jesus came to restore Fatherhood in people's lives. When disciples understand God as their Father, they see themselves differently. They're sons! As God's son, a disciple is no longer offended when the Father allows the rain to fall on a sinful neighbor's crop. What God does with rain and sun is no longer important. His walk with God demands his attention. His enemy is now a prospect for the kingdom of God. He is now free to enjoy all the blessings of God.

In essence, Jesus was saying, "No disciple will come into the fullness of his inheritance as long as he has an improper attitude toward people in the world."

When I began to understand I was a son of the heavenly Father and I had access to His warehouse, I found I could live above and beyond the limitations of the unrighteous. I had resources beyond anything a sinner could imagine.

Several years ago when I left a safe and secure pastorate, I encountered people who thought my family and I should be suffering. They thought we wouldn't have anything because our resources through a particular church had been cut off. They didn't understand I had an *inexhaustible* Source.

When the Lord launched me out into a new ministry—one in which the fullness of the Holy Spirit is proclaimed—He said, "I am going to close a door but I am going to open new doors. However, you will not be permitted to speak evil against those who persecuted you. Love will be the rule you shall follow—with your friends and especially your enemies."

As I walked in the words of the Lord, I found new provision I never knew existed. And it all came from God's vast storehouse. It would have been easy to become bitter and resentful about the situation. I must admit the circumstances didn't look good. But as I followed the rule of love, I walked into a fuller and broader ministry than I had ever known.

9 | *The Disciple's Practice of Righteousness*

"Practice makes perfect, son," my father always said. "If you learn by your mistakes, then you'll even be able to thank God for them." I thought only charismatics knew that truth until I remembered my Baptist father told me the same thing thirty years ago.

Every father gives his son an opportunity to "try his hand" at a new skill. He wisely helps, encouraging his son to improve with practice.

Some shepherds invariably hold back believers from practicing their skills at "being a Christian." Yet Jesus sent His disciples out to get practical experience (Matt. 10:5). He exhorted them to try their hand at healing the sick and casting out demons (Matt. 10:8). He also sent them out in such a way they had to totally rely upon Him as their Source (Matt. 10:9-10).

Once He sent out seventy disciples two by two (Luke 10:1). When they reported back, He was able to teach them things they needed to know (Luke 10:17-20).

Giving a disciple room to practice his righteousness and

setting him in authority over the body of Christ are not the same. Many people confuse that point. Jesus delegated authority in the church later. But the disciple who did not learn *what* to practice also did not learn *how* to grow.

Father Love Demonstrated

Jesus said, "Beware of practicing your righteousness before men to be noticed by them; otherwise you have no reward with your Father who is in heaven" (Matt. 6:1 NASB). The Greek words for "with your Father" are *para toi patri humon*. It means the disciple stands alongside his heavenly Father when he is practicing.

God looks at what the disciple is doing. To show approval, the Lord gives rewards to the disciple for his service. This is the picture of divine activity.

The plan of Jesus was very simple. The disciple was to practice his good deeds in a way which prevented others from rewarding him. Thus when the reward comes—even though it may be transmitted through another person—the disciple knows God did it. It shows the disciple that God is active in his life. His faith grows stronger. Maturity evolves.

A man who never experiences this plan thinks God has forsaken him. "I'm not good enough," the unbelieving disciple says. Doubt often takes over, binding him spiritually. In time, if the situation isn't corrected, he loses faith entirely.

Discovering the Dynamics of Sonship

Jesus declared to His disciples, "Therefore you are to be perfect *(teleioi)*, as your heavenly Father is perfect *(teleioi)*" (Matt. 5:48 NASB).

In one sense, the word *teleioi* is used to mean "complete" in the New Testament. It comes from the Greek word *telos* which means the goal or the end as one would set a goal for a race.

Paul said to the Ephesian elders, "But I do not consider my life of any account as dear to myself, in order that I may finish *(teleios)* my course, and the ministry which I received from the Lord Jesus, to testify solemnly of the gospel of the grace of God" (Acts 20:24 NASB).

According to Paul, Christian perfection was the realization of his highest for God—the development of his greatest potential. Recognizing that tremendous truth from God, Paul set out to do the will of the Father.

Jesus did the same thing. "My food is to do the will of Him who sent Me, and to accomplish His work," He said (John 4:34 NASB).

The meaning of sonship was apparent to both Jesus Christ and the apostle Paul. It meant seeing yourself in partnership with God, serving in an earthly ministry by "doing His will."

A child is essentially a self-centered person who sees life only from the perspective of his wants, his needs and his desires. There are many people—young and old—who fit this description in the body of Christ. They float from place to place looking for some anointed preacher to "bless" their lives. They only know how to receive. They have not learned how to give.

The disciple's relationship to the Father starts off at a childlike level. But the Father's higher purpose is for that relationship to grow to the point of maturity.

The Father is perfect (mature), Jesus pointed out. Just

as the Father operates in the fullness of His maturity, the disciple is expected to do the same. "You be mature, as your heavenly Father is mature," Jesus implied.

Many people have been unfortunately taught to strive to achieve the perfection of God. The impossibility of such a task has driven countless men and women of God to frustration. No wise father would do that to his son. On the contrary, he guides his son into practices which develop maturity.

The father who tries making his son into a carbon copy of himself destroys the son's individuality. Either the son rebels or he develops unhealthy dependence which hampers him throughout life. God is so much wiser than human beings. He restores His image in us through the atoning work of Jesus Christ. But He leads us further into becoming mature men—just as He is a mature Father.

Well-meaning people have often suggested that my two sons should become pastors because I'm one. It would be disastrous to plan a pastoral career for them. They must discover their own calling in Christ Jesus and mature towards it. Then their lives will be filled with maturity, as their heavenly Father's life is.

Christian maturity is leading a believer to discover his *place* in the body of Christ. When that believer realizes his highest as a son of God, he is "perfect" like his heavenly Father. That is the goal of discipleship.

Maturity as an Act of His Grace
Practicing good deeds alone does not bring a disciple into spiritual maturity. It simply gives God an

opportunity to do it in him as an act of grace. But maturity comes in mutual cooperation with God as we obey His Word.

Paul declared, "For by grace are ye saved through faith, and that not of yourselves; it is the gift of God: Not of works, lest any man should boast. For we are His workmanship, created in Christ Jesus unto good works, which God hath before ordained that we should walk in them" (Eph. 2:8-10).

This vital understanding of grace is especially important in the development of character. A disciple will not mature in Christ simply because he has united with a church or submitted himself to the oversight of another man. Those who do it with that motive are often retarded in their growth.

A disciple grows as he learns to obey the Word of God. He discovers that Jesus Christ is alive and actively involved in his life. As an act of grace, God brings the disciple's character into a new phase. Even when a disciple reaches a new level of maturity, he can look back knowing it was all a work of God.

The disciple may have relationships with many people who contribute to his life but the credit all belongs to God. The resulting work—the maturity—was a gift of God.

Three Ways to Practice Righteousness

Jesus only gave his disciples three ways for the practice of their righteousness. Yet, incredibly, the practice of the three was designed to develop the disciple's character at every level of human relationships.

The practice of giving alms developed the disciple's relationship to his fellowmen. The practice of prayer developed his relationship to God. The practice of fasting took care of his relationship to himself.

The Practice of Giving Alms

Jesus said: "When therefore you give alms, do not sound a trumpet before you, as the hypocrites do in the synagogues and in the streets, that they may be honored by men. Truly I say to you, they have their reward in full.

"But when you give alms, do not let your left hand know what your right hand is doing that your alms may be in secret; and your Father who sees in secret will repay you" (Matt. 6:2-4 NASB).

Many disciples often make the mistake of expecting the person they help to return the favor. When it's not returned, the believer looks at it as an oversight or a sign of outright rejection. Resentment toward the other person may set in, leaving the disciple disillusioned at his attempt to do "some good for somebody."

Contemporary society suggests that an invitation to dinner must be reciprocated with a dinner invitation. But Jesus told his disciples to bless people who couldn't bless them back. Such activity does something supernatural in the disciple—the Father begins to repay him. Besides the material prosperity that may come, the disciple moves into the area where God works. That's where he grows.

The Pharisee practiced his righteousness in public. He openly called attention to his actions. His reward was the public attention he received. The Pharisee understood God correctly that practicing righteousness was necessary. His deeds were good. He simply made the mistake of looking to the public for his reward—and that's all he got.

The disciple of Jesus is to practice the giving of alms before the Lord. In this way, he can look to the heavenly Father for his reward. This is the secret of giving alms—doing it in such a way that only the heavenly Father can reward the disciple.

When God responds to the believer's giving, a new sense of confidence surfaces in him. He knows the heavenly Father is at work in his life. This causes faith to grow and maturity to come.

Some confuse the "giving of alms" with "tithing." They are not the same. Tithing is an act of worship and stewardship to God. Abraham, the first man of promise, tithed to Melchizedek, priest of the most high God (Gen. 14:18-20), as an act of worship. The giving of alms is not worship. It's a generous act of love and mercy toward another person. All children of Abraham tithe their income to God. They practice righteousness by secretly giving alms above the tithe to others.

The Practice of Prayer

"And when you pray, you are not to be as the hypocrites; for they love to stand and pray in the synagogues and on the street corners, in order to be seen by men. Truly I say to you, they have their reward in full" (Matt. 6:5 NASB).

Jesus declared again that the motive of the hypocrites for praying in public was "to be seen of men." Again their only reward was having the public acknowledge them as "good, religious men."

After speaking to the motives for praying, Jesus instructed His disciples the way to pray. "But you, when you pray, go into your inner room, and when you have shut your door, pray to your Father who is in secret, and your Father who sees in secret will repay you.

"And when you are praying, do not use meaningless repetition, as the Gentiles do, for they suppose that they will be heard for their many words. Therefore do not be like them; for your Father knows what you need, before you ask Him" (Matt. 6:6-7 NASB).

In His instructions to the disciples, Jesus went so far as to even suggest the exact words to pray (verses 9-13 NASB):

"Our Father who art in heaven,
Hallowed be Thy name.
Thy Kingdom come.
Thy will be done,
On earth as it is in heaven.
Give us this day our daily bread.
And forgive us our debts, as we also have forgiven our debtors.
And do not lead us into temptation, but deliver us from evil. [For Thine is the kingdom, and the power, and the glory, forever. Amen]."

Dr. Archibald M. Hunter in *The Work and Words of Jesus* says, "When they give alms, pray and fast, the men of the kingdom will aim at reality. It is so easy to try to be superspiritual in each of these areas of practicing righteousness so that faithfulness to truth and reality in these three areas will develop the disciple. They were to learn to do these things with utter sincerity toward God and with no thought for the glory these will bring them in the eyes of men; for ostentation of that kind brings no reward from the heavenly Father."[1]

Dr. Hunter adds, "In praying, they will avoid all 'vain repetition' and 'much speaking,' " communicating truth

---

[1] Archibald M. Hunter, *The Work and Words of Jesus*, (Philadelphia: The Westminster Press, 1973), p. 65.

and sincere thoughts to God. As they approach God, they are to be concerned about three areas of their relationship to Him: (1) "the hallowing of His Name" (Matt. 6:9); (2) "the coming of His reign" (verse 10); and (3) "obedience or the doing of His will" (verse 10).[2]

The first area permits God to establish the "Father" relationship with the disciple. That brings security as the disciple understands he has a *place* with God. The Father will gloriously bless the disciple as he communes alone with Him in his prayer closet.

The second area establishes the reign of God's kingdom in his life. The kingdom of God is "righteousness, peace and joy in the Holy Ghost." Prayer releases those attributes into the disciple's life.

The third area develops the character of obedience. According to Jesus (John 15:10), obedience establishes the abiding relationship the disciple seeks with Him. In turn, "abiding" brings effective results in prayer (John 15:7).

It is evident from examining the model prayer there are three other areas which Jesus wanted to develop in His followers. They are: trust for daily provision (verse 11); forgiveness of sin (verses 12, 14, 15); and protection from future sins (verse 13).

The disciples were expected to live one day at a time (verse 11). The Children of Israel learned from the daily gift of manna (Ex. 16:1-21) the importance of expecting God's provision that way. The disciple must learn to daily appropriate everything he needs. He's also expected to use everything he receives—just as the Children of Israel did in the wilderness.

The disciple begins his day relying totally upon God to provide his needs. I call that "beginning at zero." He lives

[2]Ibid., p. 65.

that day to the fullest, returning to "zero" at the evening's close. Before retiring, everything is released back to God, who will supply new provision for the next day. The disciple's sleep is peaceful as he's strengthened for the next day's abundant living.

Besides trusting God for daily provision, the disciple was expected to develop an attitude of forgiveness. In verses 14 and 15, Jesus made it clear that disciples must forgive others in order for God to forgive them. The two principles cannot be separated. Failure to forgive others means that unresolved forgiveness remains in the disciple's life. His developing character is hindered if that occurs.

In protection from future sins, Jesus used an interesting word for temptation. It is the Greek word *peirazein*, which can mean testing as well as to seduce into sin.

For instance, Genesis 22:1 says "that God did tempt Abraham." Yet James 1:13b says that God "Himself does not tempt any one." God's tempting is a testing which works like a blacksmith's hammer to forge workmanship out of crude iron. On the other hand, the "tempting" work of Satan is to entice into sin.

There is a well-defined line between temptation and actual sin. Although temptation is not sin, it can lead to sin. For instance, James 1:14-15 says, "But each one is tempted when he is carried away and enticed by his own lust. Then when lust has conceived, it gives birth to sin. . ." (NASB). Temptation is the birthplace for sin. James says the finished product is "death."

The Practice of Fasting

Fasting is where a disciple comes into wholeness with

himself, bringing his appetites under control. Jesus didn't say "if you fast." He said "when." That indicates he expected each disciple to make fasting a normal part of his Christian experience—like prayer or giving alms.

"When you fast, anoint your head and wash your face so that you may not be seen fasting by men, but by your Father who is in secret; and your Father who sees in secret will repay you" (Matt. 6:17-18 NASB).

According to Leviticus 16:31, all Jewish men had to afflict their souls on the day of atonement. They could not eat, drink, bathe, anoint themselves, wear sandals or indulge in conjugal intercourse. Fasting was a matter of personal discipline so that their complete attention would be directed toward God. They would not be distracted by any other circumstances.

In Matthew 4:3, Jesus fasted during the ordeal of His testing. In Daniel 9:3, Daniel fasted as he waited on a word from God. In Judges 20:26, the entire nation of Israel fasted after the disaster of the civil war with Benjamin. In 1 Samuel 7:6, Samuel called the people to fast because they followed after Baal and sinned. After he had preached the Word of God in Ninevah, Jonah saw that the people entered into a fast as they considered their sin.

Bondages are often broken during fasts, releasing new freedom into the disciple's life. When the body is disciplined, the spirit and mind have greater freedom to respond to God. It is evident that Jesus emphasized *personal discipline* as the most effective means of bringing a disciple into maturity. Personal discipline—reflected in the act of fasting—is more effective than discipline that can be exercised one man over another.

Jesus instructed two practices when the disciple fasted. First, he said, is to anoint his head with oil (Matt. 6:17). A supernatural work takes place when the disciple anoints his head. Oil—symbolic of the anointing work of the Holy Spirit—crystallizes the disciple's consecration in realizing the purposes of God in the fast. Disciples have been known to experience a fresh outpouring of the Holy Spirit in their bodies during the ceremony of anointing with oil.

Second, Jesus instructed the disciple should wash his face. By this act, the believer presents a clean, well-groomed side to people—yet all the while laying out his act of obedience before God and not man. This act of obedience, according to John 15:7, brings corresponding rewards from the Lord.

Seven Principles for the Practice of Righteousness
The golfer who excels in the sport must develop good habits in his stance and swing if he expects to achieve a good score. Forming good habits is necessary in acquiring any skill. Without them, the apprentice will never achieve the excellence of the "pros."

Jesus was training pros. Each one was an important part of His plan for world evangelism and body ministry. Remarkably the Lord Jesus didn't leave a stone unturned in explaining the rules of the game. After showing the disciple three practice areas, He gave seven principles to follow to enhance his skills as he practiced. Following these seven principles will mean the difference between success and failure in the practice of righteousness.

Liberality with the Father's Blessings
"Do not lay up for yourselves treasures upon earth,

where moth and rust destroy, and where thieves break in and steal. But lay up for yourselves treasures in heaven, where neither moth nor rust destroys, and where thieves do not break in or steal; for where your treasure is, there will your heart be also" (Matt. 6:19-21 NASB).

In these Scriptures, Jesus clearly demonstrated that His disciples must establish the proper value system and set priorities.

My wife, our two sons and I arrived in Spain in September, 1965, with a truckload of expensive furniture, china and other personal objects. Apprehensive about our new missionary life, we were clinging to every possible memory of the comfortable life we had left behind in the States.

Yet before we could even get the moving van unloaded, four terrible days struck. Torrential rains—caused by a severe north Atlantic storm—flooded the area , engulfing the moving van. It was several days before the raging waters subsided.

When the van was finally opened, my wife crumpled to the ground weeping. The family possessions appeared totally ruined in their washed-out condition. Four-year-old William walked over to his mother. "Don't cry, mama," he said, caressing her tear-drenched cheek with his tiny hands. "Don't worry about the furniture. We still have each other."

The words of truth gripped us all. My wife stood up, straightened her dress and began to direct the unloading of the "remains" into our house. God had dramatically permitted the Ligons to learn the importance of this principle.

The disciple dependent upon material possessions is not free to help others. He doesn't have the discipline to handle the abundance of resources the Father wants to give through him. If God blessed him with an abundant material supply, he would "spend it on his pleasures" (James 4:3b).

Such a disciple is unable to grasp the principle of "sowing seeds" explained by Paul in 2 Corinthians 9:10-15. Ignorance of this principle will prevent the disciple from giving alms. He will always feel he must meet another need in his own life, before helping someone else.

Paul speaks to this very situation in Philippians 4:11-13: "For I have learned to be content in whatever circumstances I am. I know how to get along with humble means, and I also know how to live in prosperity; in any and every circumstance I have learned the secret of being filled and going hungry, both of having abundance and suffering need. I can do all things through Him who strengthens me" (NASB).

Jesus made it clear His disciples were to be delivered from the material things of life. He declared:

"The light of the body is the eye: if therefore thine eye be single, thy whole body shall be full of light. But if thine eye be evil, thy whole body shall be full of darkness. If therefore the light that is in thee be darkness, how great is that darkness!

"No man can serve two masters: for either he will hate the one, and love the other; or else he will hold to the one, and despise the other. Ye cannot serve God and mammon" (Matt. 6:22-24).

The Greek word for single is *haplos*. In Romans 12:8,

Paul urged his friends to give liberally (*haplos*). In 2 Corinthians 9:13, he reminded the church at Corinth of the liberality (*haplotes*) of the churches in Macedonia. He also referred to their own liberal (*haplous*) distribution to all men.

On the other hand, the Greek word for evil is *poneros*, which means "to grudge." In the Septuagint, the Greek translation of the Old Testament, the word *haplos* is used to translate the word evil as in Deut. 15:9, "thine eye is evil."

The disciple with the single (generous) eye will have a body full of light. The one with the evil (grudging) eye will have a body filled with darkness. His darkness is actually "great" because he thinks he's walking in the light when actually his darkness has blinded him to the truth.

Jesus' lesson is obvious. The disciple will be able to minister to others only to the degree he's free from a grudging spirit. In verse 24, Jesus showed that the disciple who failed to develop a generous attitude toward other people will be devoted to mammon more than God. He personified the word "mammon" using it like the personality of another god. Thus, the disciple who doesn't practice giving alms has divided loyalties.

Faith in the Father's Support
The disciple who doesn't understand the principle of the Father's support in all his activities will not be free to give alms, pray or fast.

"Take no thought for your life" (Matt. 6:25b). The Greek word for thought is *merimnate*. It means "worry with much anxiety." The NASB renders that verse, "do not be anxious for your life."

The disciple who enters into the practice of righteousness can do so with complete faith in the heavenly Father's provision. He doesn't have to worry about food (verse 25), clothing (verse 28), or even the length of his life (verse 27).

There is ample reason for the disciple not to engage in worry. If he understands the nature of his sonship, he realizes the heavenly Father has already made provision for him as he engages in the work of the Kingdom.

Demonstrating this fact, Jesus sent the seventy disciples out without money. They returned to Jesus rejoicing. The disciple recognizes that sonship means the heavenly Father will provide for his needs as part of their partnership.

Jesus expected his disciples to devote themselves to more important things. He said, "But seek first His kingdom and His righteousness, and all these things shall be added to you" (Matt. 6:33 NASB). If the disciple is preoccupied with himself, he'll overlook ministry to others. His prayers will be limited to his own needs. He won't exercise proper discipline over his own body.

In developing this attitude of faith in the Father's support, Jesus showed that both birds and flowers (verses 26-29) receive their life from God, living out their time without worry. He noted that worry over material possessions was the way of the Gentiles or unbelievers (verse 32).

The Father is able to release an abundance of supplies to the disciple who devotes himself toward maintaining a right relationship with God and "seeking first" His Kingdom.

Freedom from Unjust Criticism

"Do not judge lest you be judged yourselves. For in the way you judge, you will be judged; and by your standard of measure, it shall be measured to you.

"And why do you look at the speck in your brother's eye, but do not notice the log that is in your own eye? Or how can you say to your brother, 'Let me take the speck out of your eye,' and behold, the log is in your own eye?

"You hypocrite, first take the log out of your own eye, and then you will see clearly enough to take the speck out of your brother's eye" (Matt. 7:1-5 NASB).

Critical judgment is no doubt one of the most vulnerable areas in a disciple's life. Jesus knew His disciples would wrestle with this thorny problem. Thus He explained a principle which would either lead to divisions between disciples or build right relationships.

Countless mistakes have been made in efforts to disciple men. A person who sets himself up as an example for others to follow, as did the apostle Paul, must be able to say as Paul did, "I am the chief of sinners."

Jesus demonstrated the best grounds upon which a person can correct the behavior of another brother is that of mutual recognition of sins. The disciple who permits himself to become judgmental will find it difficult to practice righteousness. He will start deciding what persons need the blessings, love and forgiveness of God instead of leaving that choice to the Holy Spirit. In the process, the Holy Spirit's work is usurped.

When my family and I returned from Spain in 1971, we learned on arrival that my wife's only brother had terminal cancer. At thirty years of age, he was facing death—unprepared to meet God.

My wife's first response was to go to her prayer closet. "I don't think God's going to hear those prayers," I said harshly one day. "You know the life your brother's lived." My words judged, preventing me from praying effectively for his salvation.

"It's not for me to judge his behavior," my wife responded. "I only know he needs to be saved, healed and filled with God's Spirit. My Bible tells me that God hears my prayers."

She was right. God did hear those prayers and, in spite of my disobedience, gave me the privilege of baptizing my wife's brother in water. I learned a great lesson that day about ministry. A person must be prepared to forgive literally "anything" when his actions encourage another person to trust God.

In another sense, there is a danger in getting to know the faults of other persons. Often people are judged and rejected on the basis of information others have about them. "I thought he was a Christian until I found out. . ." is a common expression among many church folks.

Prayer meetings can actually turn into gossip sessions. "Pray for Brother Jones; I understand he's running around with another woman" is a prayer request I've heard at meetings. Many disciples don't know how to handle private information about others. God can't use them fully until they learn this vital lesson.

Many believers would like to share their fears and failures with compassionate brothers and sisters but can't. They fear that such confession will lead to judgmental rejection, or even worse—open gossip in the community.

Therefore, the disciple must begin to practice

"acceptance" and confidentiality of the brother about whom he knows secrets. This "acceptance" can many times aid a weaker disciple in overcoming guilt from the past. By enabling a weaker disciple to function more fully as God intended, the body of Christ will be greatly strengthened.

Wisdom in the Practice of Righteousness

"Do not give what is holy to dogs, and do not throw your pearls before swine, lest they trample them under their feet, and turn and tear you to pieces" (Matt. 7:6 NASB).

The words of Jesus referring to others as "dogs" seems almost harsh at first glance. Yet it was common in His day for Jews to refer to Gentiles or heathens as "dogs."

In this verse, Jesus described a scene in which a disciple shared a choice word of Scripture or a personal experience with the Lord with a person who openly scorned his beliefs. A disciple should be discerning enough before he shares an experience to know whether the hearer will respect his experience or not.

As a pastor, I have known of many situations when a Christian was diagnosed as having a serious disease. Later that person received a miracle of healing and returned to the doctor for confirmation. On getting that confirmation, the believer testified of his miraculous healing to the doctor, making demands that the physician agree "it was all the work of the Lord."

If the doctor is a believer in the miraculous works of Jesus, he can share in his patient's joy. But if he only believes in the scientific method of healing, he's placed in the position of evaluating the Holy Spirit's work with limited natural reasoning. Paul said the natural man can't understand the things of the Spirit (1 Cor. 2:14).

God never intended that His miraculous works of healing or His gifts of the Spirit should be evaluated by persons of unbelief—regardless of their training or profession. Thus the disciple needs to practice the wisdom of the Lord lest he "throw his pearls before swine."

Knowledge of God's Plan of Provision

"Ask, and it shall be given to you; seek, and you shall find; knock, and it shall be opened to you. For every one who asks receives, and he who seeks finds, and to him who knocks it shall be opened.

"Or what man is there among you, when his son shall ask him for a loaf, will give him a stone? Or if he shall ask for a fish, he will not give him a snake, will he?

"If you then, being evil, know how to give good gifts to your children, how much more shall your Father who is in heaven give what is good to those who ask Him" (Matt. 7:7-11 NASB).

During more than twenty years of ministry, I have known some mighty prayer warriors who never understood this kind of access to the heavenly Father was available to them. Somehow they thought Jesus' words in Matthew 6:32—"your heavenly Father knoweth that ye have need of all these things"—prevented them from specifically asking for things.

During our six years in Spain, my wife and I worked with some twenty other missionary couples who were assigned mission funds from the board back in the United States. These funds were distributed annually to all missionaries who held equal rank in the mission.

Budgets and requisitions were prepared annually to

request funds and decide their distribution for the next year. Some were more diligent than others in planning their work and asking for funds. Others were less concerned with planning and using funds. Those who didn't ask—who didn't verbalize their needs—were often overlooked.

In looking at verses 7-11, I understand Jesus saying to these future church leaders: "Men, don't forget to use the requisition system as a way of supplying your needs while you're working. Develop good habits, make a continual and daily practice of it. Prepare a list of the needs for your work and your family. Name them one by one to the Father in prayer. This is the way it works in the kingdom—ask, seek, knock."

Excitement comes when the disciple discovers this principle works. His life is strengthened as he asks the Father "in secret" for provisions, expecting them to be supplied. As provisions come through various sources, the disciple recognizes they originated in God. His practice of prayer matures him in the Lord.

I have watched my wife ask for a specific amount of money just to give to someone in need. Within days, that amount would be supplied. "Thank you, Lord," I've heard her say, "I'll deliver it to the person today."

At times, she's received more than she asked for. She knew the extra was for her. God had supplied the other person's need and rewarded her in the process. She had shared in the prosperity of her prayer.

In Luke 11:5-8, Jesus showed that persistence in prayer pays off. The disciple should therefore make his request known to God. That demonstrates responsible stewardship. The disciple who continually practices that kind of stewardship will discover it pays to practice the principle of asking.

Freedom to Put Others First

"Therefore whatever you want others to do for you, do so for them, for this is the Law and the Prophets" (Matt. 7:12 NASB).

This principle strengthens the disciple in prayer, giving alms and fasting. Disciples frequently have to make a decision regarding another person without hearing a specific "word from the Lord." In 1 Corinthians 7:25, Paul acknowledged he didn't have a word from the Lord on a particular matter. Yet he told the brethren what he thought should be done. He was secure enough in Christ that he trusted his conscience and the inner witness of his spirit.

This principle will aid the disciple in making the right decision under most any circumstance. If a disciple doesn't have a direct word from God, he should "do for the other person what he'd like for the other person to do for him."

It is a positive affirmation of life, which the disciple should adopt in his own Christian experience. It reflects the personality of the Father who according to Romans 5:8 "demonstrates His own love toward us, in that while we were yet sinners, Christ died for us" (NASB).

Faith to Follow Difficult Paths

"Enter by the narrow gate; for the gate is wide, and the way is broad that leads to destruction, and many are those who enter by it. For the gate is small, and the way is narrow that leads to life, and few are those who find it" (Matt. 7:13-14 NASB).

This seventh principle reflects the life of a disciple who

has reached the height of Christian maturity, according to Jesus' words in Matthew 5:10-12. It is not easy to choose the road of sacrifice when an easier choice would possibly go unnoticed. Every disciple is faced with such choices daily.

It is much easier to smile indulgently at the crude jokes of a co-worker than to bear witness of the love of Jesus. Some Christians feel the "narrow road" is only for the more dedicated. Yet Jesus made it plain that taking the difficult but committed route was for all believers. After all, He was going to choose apostles from His disciples.

Says Elton Trueblood in *The Company of the Committed*, "As we study carefully the strategy employed by Christ, we are forced to conclude that the crucial step was that by which disciples were turned into apostles. It was necessary, of course, to have disciples first, because there had to be some reservoir of human resources on which to draw before the actual penetration of the world could begin."[3]

That kind of discipleship creates men out of boys.

Apostles are God's men who've learned to walk the narrow road regardless of who walks with them. They forged ahead with the message of Christ burning in their hearts. They couldn't compromise the Word of God because they'd become "bond slaves" to it. Their conscience bore record that the broad way was the road of compromise.

It has always been easy to follow the way of the crowds. That's the broad way. But it requires diligence to stay on the path of righteousness—the Jesus way. Few are found on that road. Yet those who are have discovered the secret of discipleship.

[3]Elton Trueblood, *The Company of the Committed*, (New York: Harper and Row, 1961), p. 70.

10 | *The Fruit of a False Prophet*

As Jesus drew to a close with the "Sermon on the Mount," He unexpectedly shifted (Matt. 7:15) into a warning about false prophets. Many have suggested the material on false prophets seems totally unrelated to the teaching on Christian discipleship.

Yet on closer examination, it is obvious that Jesus clearly understood what He was doing. His disciples were going to guide the formative days of the Christian church. It would be *essential* then that they be able to discern between the true and false prophets.

It would be no problem spotting an Elmer Gantry type, who comes into town for the sole purpose of "fleecing" the flock. But what about the kind of man like Saul? He began as an anointed man of God but gradually moved away under the influence of a seducing spirit. Church history is laced with the stories of men like Saul.

Even today in this fresh, twentieth-century move of the Holy Spirit, false doctrines and false "christs" have surfaced repeatedly. Jesus himself considered it important enough to include in His basic message to His disciples. If it was important then, it is vital now.

False Prophets in the Old Testament

The Hebrew people were well acquainted with false prophets. It was Jeremiah who said, "An appalling and horrible thing has happened in the land: The prophets prophesy falsely, and the priests rule on their *own* authority; and my people love it so! But what will you do at the end of it?" (Jer. 5:30-31 NASB).

Three alarming notes deserve attention in Jeremiah's cry. First, false prophecy was operating among the people of God. Second, priests were ruling by an authority not established by God. And third, God's people were showing they liked to have men rule over them.

When I first came into the charismatic dimension, I heard much about the prophetic word within the church. The verse quoted most frequently as a guide to discerning the false prophet was Deuteronomy 18:22.

"When a prophet speaks in the name of the Lord, if the thing does not come about or come true, that is the thing which the Lord has not spoken. The prophet has spoken it presumptuously; you shall not be afraid of him" (NASB).

Oddly enough, some leaders of modern-day New Testament churches proceeded to establish guidelines given the Children of Israel as the basis for recognizing a false prophet today. If a genuine prophet was supposed to be correct 100 percent of the time, how would people be able to keep up with his record to know?

I was often troubled by that "prophet-judging standard," even though I sometimes used Deuteronomy

18:22 to warn people about false prophets. My uneasiness increased even more when I heard people say a certain Bible teacher's interpretation of Scripture could be followed without question. Many people believed certain Bible teachers didn't make mistakes.

The men of Berea weren't like that. Luke says that they "received the word with great eagerness, examining the Scriptures daily, to see whether these things [taught by Paul and Silas] were true" (Acts 17:11 NASB).

This discernment seemed basic with many Old Testament prophets. Ezekiel was gifted with the ability to know the false from the true (Ezek. 22:25-26). Micah demonstrated prophetically that God had shown him to discern the work of a false witness (Micah 3:5). Zephaniah said that the prophets had become "reckless, treacherous men" (Zeph. 3:4).

The role of the true prophet of God was not easy. When Ahab and Jehoshaphat formed an alliance to capture Ramoth-Gilead from Syria, the prophet Micaiah stood against 400 false prophets. Jehoshaphat had requested that inquiry be made before the battle to know "the word of the Lord" (2 Chron. 18:4-5). As a result of taking his stand, Micaiah ended up in prison on bread and water.

The law of Moses (Deut. 13:5) called for severe punishment for those who prophesied falsely. Yet, it was the true prophet of God who was stoned, imprisoned and often executed. Jesus made reference to this when he called the scribes and Pharisees "sons of those who murdered the prophets" (Matt. 23:31 NASB).

According to Jesus, the scribes and Pharisees were saying if they had lived in the former days of their fathers (Matt. 23:29-30), they "would not have been partners with them in shedding the blood of the prophets" (NASB).

The scribes and Pharisees thought they knew a man of God when they saw one. They most certainly counted themselves in that elite number while excluding the Lord Jesus Christ.

Cults have splintered off from the mainstream of Christianity in just the same way. Those who followed their founders were confident too that they "knew a prophet when they saw one." The results, however, of these movements from the time of Jesus until today show these people were sadly mistaken.

False Prophets in the New Testament

The New Testament did not leave the issue of the false prophet in the dark. Paul and Barnabas met a false prophet at Cyprus and dealt with his deception (Acts 13:4-12). Many false prophets have gone out into the world, according to the apostle John (1 John 4:1). Peter warned the brethren that there would be "false teachers among you, who will secretly introduce destructive heresies" (2 Pet. 2:1 NASB).

Peter's warning is especially noteworthy. These false teachers were "among them"—that is, they were in the local church. Yet they worked introducing their heresies "secretly."

Before leaving the work at Ephesus (Acts 20:29), Paul warned the elders that when he departed "savage wolves" would begin to infiltrate the flock. Moreover, from their own ranks, men would rise up "speaking perverse things" to draw away disciples after them (verse 30).

Paul's words of advice were that they keep their eyes on the Lord and stay in the Word of God. He explained if they obeyed the Word of God, it would build them up and insure that they receive their inheritance among the fellowship of believers (verse 32).

There is no evidence that Paul tried to do anything else to prepare them to deal with these false teachers. He didn't organize any credentials committees or sergeants-at-arms. He simply left, trusting the Holy Spirit to carry on the work of God among the Ephesians (verse 36). It is this kind of basic faith in God that does not hinder the ministry of the Holy Spirit. He alone is able to maintain balance among sensible men of God.

The False Prophet as Jesus Saw Him

Jesus unveiled some specific guidelines for evaluating a prophet of God, listing eight characteristics which eventually show up at the final judgment. First, he said, false prophets wear sheep's clothing (Matt. 7:15). They are deceptive persons but their outward appearance is just like the average church-goer.

Zechariah prophesied that the day would come when false prophets would be ashamed of their false visions and would stop wearing "a hairy robe in order to deceive" (Zech. 13:4 NASB). Clearly, the practice of a false prophet was to imitate the dress of God's prophet. There is nothing wrong with a prophet dressing like a prophet—whether it's a "hairy robe" or a Brooks Brothers suit. But Jesus didn't want His disciples to be fooled by a prophet's outward dress.

Jesus said: "Do men gather grapes of thorns or figs of thistles? Even so every good tree bringeth forth good fruit; but a corrupt tree bringeth forth evil fruit. A good tree cannot bring forth evil fruit, neither can a corrupt tree bring forth good fruit. Every tree that bringeth not forth good fruit is hewn down, and cast into the fire" (Matt. 7:16-19).

It is evident from Jesus' choice of words that a false prophet would not bear genuine fruit of the Spirit—love, joy, peace, etc. Obviously, the false prophet would manifest one personality in an assembly of believers and yet another personality elsewhere. As a corrupt person, he could not manifest all the time the "good" which only God can give. His fruit would eventually bring forth evil.

The true nature of the prophet's work would be revealed when the fruit burst forth on the tree he was cultivating. That could either be his own life or the work he was promoting. The process takes time—even years—but eventually the fruit reveals what kind of tree it came from.

Third, the false prophet will even speak the correct language to make himself sound like a genuine prophet (verse 21). He can say, "Lord, Lord" with great gusto and enthusiasm.

I frequently hear of some well-known personality being identified as a Christian simply because he used an expression identified with Christian people. Nothing could be further from the truth. Using the right vocabulary means nothing to God. Jesus said the only way to get into His Kingdom was to do "the will of my Father which is in heaven" (Matt. 7:21b).

Fourth, the false prophet will be able to prophesy (verse 22a). On more than one occasion, I have received copies of printed prophecies which had been originally spoken in meetings throughout the country. Assuming that all of the prophecies had been tested and accepted at the specific meetings as genuine words from God for the people in attendance, there was no scriptural basis for printing and distributing the prophecies as "God's word" for the entire body of Christ.

Prophecy distributed in that fashion as a "word from God to be obeyed" equates the prophetic word with the Holy Scriptures. A person borders on the extreme when he uses prophecy in this way. Although the Lord gave prophecy only for "edification, exhortation and comfort" (1 Cor. 14:3), current trends lean toward equating it to the authority of Scripture.

The false prophet, Jesus said, will actually point to his prophetic work as justification for his acceptance into the kingdom of heaven. By avoiding the atoning work of Christ in favor of his own prophetic work, the false prophet usurps the place of authority only given to Jesus Christ. He is, therefore, false.

Revelation 22:18-19 says, "I testify to everyone who hears the words of the prophecy of this book: if anyone adds to them, God shall add to him the plagues which are written in this book; and if anyone takes away from the words of the book of this prophecy, God will take away his part from the tree of life and from the holy city, which are written in this book" (NASB).

Fifth, the false prophet will also be able to cast out demons (verse 22b). There is a valid ministry in deliverance. The "seventy" disciples found that out when Jesus sent them out to minister (Luke 10:17).

But Jesus showed that the false prophet will point to his power to deliver people from the clutches of demonic forces as evidence of his credibility as an anointed prophet of God. Casting out demons does not give any man grounds for justification before God. Anyone who believes in the authority vested in the name of Jesus can cast out demons. He is working *for* the Kingdom, but he may not be *in* the Kingdom.

Sixth, the false prophet will be able to work miracles (verse 22c). The operation of miracles within the church is necessary. Hebrews 2:4 reveals that God used miracles to confirm His redemptive work in Jesus Christ. However, the Lord Jesus wanted His disciples to avoid using this consideration as a way of evaluating a man's validity.

Moses found out that false prophets can sometimes reproduce miracles (Exod. 7:9, 11, 12 and 8:7) more than cnce in his efforts to persuade the Pharaoh in Egypt to release the Children of Israel. Pharaoh used the test of supernatural demonstrations, in turn, to challenge the validity of Moses' authority.

Scores of church members run after prophets who demonstrate miraculous powers, while never checking to see if their "fruit" agrees with their supernatural work. Deception easily enters into the church through this door.

Seventh, the false prophet is a lawless person (verse 23). The key word here is "iniquity," which is more correctly translated "lawlessness." To be lawless is to refuse to recognize God's ordained authority. While some false prophets assume absolute authority over believers, others refuse to recognize any delegated authority at all.

A false prophet will not recognize and respect the authority of brothers given to keep him in balance. He is a self-centered maverick whose lawless attitude is often expressed in dictatorial ways. He has the "I've heard from God and nobody will tell me what to do" attitude.

Eight, the false prophet is a person who hears the Word of the Lord but doesn't act upon it (Matt. 7:26-27). In this case, the false prophet is also like the son in Jesus' parable (Matt. 21:28-30) who tells his father he will obey his command but never does.

Jesus was speaking to the chief priests and elders in the temple when he gave this parable. He saw the religious leaders of his day "hearing" the Word of God but putting their own interpretation to it. Their "practice" did not agree with the written Word of the Father. Therefore, they were "hearing" but not "acting."

Anyone who hears the words of Jesus but doesn't act is like a "foolish man, who built his house upon the sand," the Scripture says. The wind and rain came against the house and it fell. It was not constructed on a solid foundation.

False Prophets Working from Within

A blind-sided view of false prophets exists in sectors of the church. Some believe that a false prophet comes deliberately to deceive with his great knowledge, deep wisdom and eloquent words. Such is not the case.

Paul said to the elders at Ephesus, "From among your own selves men will arise, speaking perverse things, to draw away the disciples after them" (Acts 20:30 NASB). Thus, it is clear that deception which scatters the people of God can come from within more powerfully than without.

It is extremely difficult for a disciple to detect false teaching in a Bible teacher he admires. He struggles emotionally. His spirit says the teaching is in error even though his heart says his favorite teacher couldn't be wrong. He is like a young suitor carried away by the feminine charms of his beloved. He is blinded to the deception of her ways. His ability to function wisely is impaired.

For the disciple, the relationship began on a note of genuine truth which the teacher established with sound biblical exposition. Then, like young lovers enraptured by the devoted words they shared, they moved gradually into error. At first, the changes were so minute no one, not even the all-knowing teacher, suspected.

By the time heresy is evident, it has become so much a part of teacher and disciple they can't see the problem. They are now part of it.

David Berg: A Haunting Example of Deception

Nowhere in the present church age is there a more complete example of a man and a group turning from the truth into heresy as did David Berg and the Children of God. In fact, a recent *Christianity Today* article called them, "Children of God: Disciples of Deception."

Chuck and Bonnie Watson weren't looking to be deceived when they joined the group. After all, they had been Christians for most of their lives. Bonnie had been to Bible school, while Chuck had been a "system preacher." Yet, like a moth to a flame, they were drawn to COG.

And with them went thousands of others. Some almost dead from drugs. Others just back from war-ravaged Viet Nam. A few had been thieves and ex-Mafia members. There were hippies from Haight-Ashbury and rosy-cheeked kids just like your next-door neighbor's.

What was the drawing power that brought all of these people together? Who could cause them to turn their backs on family, friends and loved ones? Many gave up security and good careers to join a motley group of castaways revolting against the world systems—all for

Jesus.

The drawing power was a charismatic leader, David Berg.

A highly trained, one-time fundamentalist gospel preacher, Berg became convinced—after years in the system—that the church bore no resemblance to the Bible's original design. "It was a once-a-week meeting place for a powerless bunch of hypocrites who were unprepared for the tribulation," he said.

Berg had an incredible natural ability to work with people, young and old alike. He spoke their language, thought their thoughts, fired their dreams. He was completely believable, a man without guile. Berg believed that he had God's answer for serious disciples of his day.

Together with his wife and four teen-agers, they instilled a sense of purpose and belonging in young people who were empty. In short, they gave people a *place* to belong. Society and church had let them down but David Berg never would.

That was how the whole movement began in 1968. But along the way, the 50 members of the California-based "Teens for Christ" grew into the 5,000-member worldwide movement called the Children of God. David Berg, the man with God's vision for today, became "Moses David," prophet, psychic and husband of five wives.

Chuck and Bonnie, products of the church, became "Amos" and "Ruth," participants in a movement blindly following the revelations of one man. A man who became answerable to no one.

And what could have been a genuine movement from God slowly turned into error. So casual was the error that people trained in the Bible couldn't recognize it until they too were in error. From a group born in strict adherence to biblical truths, COG departed into spiritism, astrology, sexual immorality and the Moslem religion—yet still proclaiming the name of Jesus.

What happened? How did dedicated, sold-out, well-meaning people like the Watsons get into spiritual deception? What was the lure? Who was at fault?

From the Watsons' viewpoint, they saw Berg as a man who loved God and desired to put the real truth of the Bible into practice. He identified serious problems in the church system and wanted to correct them.

COG disciples believed that Berg had the answers to the perplexing questions in their lives. These disciples loved God and thought they could serve Him through COG. So committed were these disciples, they were willing to die for their beliefs.

But both the disciples and Berg wandered into absolute rebellion against the God they so much loved. Totally deceived, Berg became like Saul of old—given over to an evil spirit, the victim of pride and rebellion.

His disciples had started out with him seeking the life devoted to Christ. They ended up hopelessly trapped in a cult. The example of Berg and the Children of God has been repeated numerous times in every generation. It is the story of a charismatic figure answerable to no one. The end result is spiritual deception.

Walter R. Martin in *The Kingdom of the Cults* defined a "cult" as "any religious group which differs significantly in some one or more respects as to belief or practice, from those religious groups which are regarded as the normative expressions of religion in our total culture."[1]

He further stated that it could be defined as "a group of

[1]Walter R. Martin, *The Kingdom of the Cults*, (Minneapolis: Bethany Fellowship, Inc., 1970), p. 11.

people gathered about a specific person or person's interpretation of the Bible. For example, Jehovah's Witnesses are, for the most part, followers of the interpretations of Charles T. Russell and J.F. Rutherford."

Martin has listed four psychological attitudes of cultists which make it difficult for them to walk with other people. First, the cultist is close-minded. This is due to the fact that he is completely committed to the authority pattern of his organization.

Second, he identifies his dislike of other expressions of Christianity with the Christians who do not accept his beliefs. Thus, he tends to reject fellowship with people who do not agree with him.

Third, cultists manifest an intolerance for any position but their own. Martin pointed out that is why people like the Mormon prophet Joseph Smith, Russell of the Jehovah's Witnesses and Mary Baker Eddy of Christian Science all insisted that their pronouncements were direct revelations from God. Such revelations make any other teaching unacceptable.

Fourth, there is the "factor of isolation." They become so committed to their teachings and their teachers that they are spiritually blind to any error in their ranks. Thus Jehovah's Witnesses are blind to the fact that Judge Rutherford insisted that Abraham, Isaac and Jacob would return to earth before the close of the 1920s.[2]

[2]Ibid., pp. 24, 25, 26.

11 | *The Fruit of a True Prophet*

"Beware of the false prophets, who come to you in sheep's clothing, but inwardly are ravenous wolves. You will know them by their *fruits*. Grapes are not gathered from thorn bushes, nor figs from thistles, are they? Even so, every good tree bears good fruit; but the rotten tree bears bad fruit" (Matt. 7:15-17 NASB, italics mine).

A prophet is judged by the fruit in his life just as a fruit tree is judged by the kind and quality of fruit it produces.

Emphasis was placed in the Greek upon knowing (*epignosesthe*). The verb (*ginosko*) means to know. But the addition of *epi* emphasized that the ability of the disciple to know a false prophet was made full. "You will fully know."

He talked about fruits (plural) in verses 16 and 20, and fruit (singular) in verses 17, 18, 19. "A good tree bears good fruit (singular)," Jesus said. "You will know them (plural) by their fruits (plural)."

Each prophet, then, was to be known by the fruit (as a

cluster of grapes) on the branches of his life.

Fruit bears in season. Many trees don't produce fruit the first season after planting. It takes time to cultivate fruit.

The church has made a great mistake in putting men into responsible positions of leadership too quickly. A person from the drug scene or entertainment world can confess of a conversion experience one day and be introduced the next day giving his testimony. The "sensationalism" of his dramatic conversion is capitalized on by the church in an effort to convince others to accept Christ. Too easily, the unsuspecting church members can assume the novice to be an approved church leader. The church has been embarrassed by novices who slipped back into their old ways after being pushed to the front by eager-beavers.

Paul said not to put a new convert in leadership "lest he become conceited and fall into the condemnation incurred by the devil" (1 Tim. 3:6 NASB). He added in verse seven a leader "must have a good reputation with those outside the church, so that he may not fall into reproach and the snare of the devil" (NASB).

It takes time to change old, ingrained habits. Jesus kept his new converts (disciples) with Him for three years before they were released into leadership roles. In the three years, they were ready to be anointed by the Holy Spirit for more responsible ministry.

People who enjoy the "dramatic" always gather around an exciting new convert, vicariously enjoying his charisma. His new "fame" in the church drives the new believer to excitement, leaving behind the less attractive task of forming new habits. He is in danger of being snared by the old habits which had only been suppressed for a season.

Christ in You

"I need help," the man said anxiously, a grim expression etched on his face. The worship service had just ended and the man had cornered me as I turned to leave the platform. "My Christian experience is just going sour," he mumbled, shaking his head.

"What seems to be going wrong, brother?" I asked, placing my hand on his shoulder.

"Oh, I don't know," he said exasperated, "I just don't seem to have any peace or joy anymore. Situations continually upset me. I don't seem to have the patience I once had with people. It looks so useless for me. I never will have any fruit in my life."

The man's symptoms were ones I had seen frequently. Unknowingly, he had set impossible goals for himself. He wanted to be like Jesus—perfectly handling every situation he faced in life. Condemnation stalked his steps every time he "blew it."

The brother was making two serious mistakes about the Christian life. First, he was expecting to achieve a Christ-like life through Bible study, prayer and discipline. He failed to understand the mystery of this life which is "Christ in you, the hope of glory" (Col. 1:27). It wasn't his life *made* mature but the life of Christ matured *in* him.

The only thing the disciple could expect to achieve in his body was the dying power of Jesus. "Always carrying about in the body the dying of Jesus, that the life of Jesus also may be manifested in our body" (2 Cor. 4:10 NASB).

While he was trying to develop as a "good Christian," the Holy Spirit was working to bring death to his carnal nature.

Second, he failed to recognize the difference between the "fruit of our labors" and the "fruit of the Holy Spirit."

Paul said, "For to me, to live is Christ, and to die is gain. But if I am to live on in the flesh, this will mean *fruitful* labor for me; and I do not know which to choose" (Phil. 1:21-22 NASB, italics mine). Paul's fruitful labor was bringing converts into maturity and founding strong churches. Accordingly, God responds to that kind of work with rewards (Phil. 3:13-14).

The apostle had fruit of the Spirit present in his life (Gal. 5:22-23) just like any other disciple. God gave him that as a gift of the Holy Spirit, enabling him to minister the life and character of Christ to others. He couldn't do anything to achieve that except recognize by faith that the fruit was resident *within* him.

The Ministry of the Christ

Many fail to recognize the present-day ministry of Jesus in their lives. Thus the impossibility of their own efforts to be like Jesus often drives believers to defeat. Once provoked over a situation, it's easier to react than abide in Christ.

Hebrews 8:6 declares that Jesus "has obtained a more excellent *ministry*, by as much as He is also the mediator of a better covenant, which has been enacted on better promises" (NASB, italics mine).

Jesus has now "taken His seat at the right hand of the throne of the Majesty in the heavens, a *minister* in the sanctuary, and in the true tabernacle, which the Lord pitched not man" (Heb. 8:1-2 NASB, italics mine).

"Therefore, holy brethren, partakers of a heavenly calling," says Hebrews 3:1, "consider Jesus, the Apostle and High Priest of our confession" (NASB).

When the disciple understands the present-day ministry of Jesus, it will revolutionize his walk in the Spirit. To better understand Jesus' ministry today, the disciple must look at the priesthood of Aaron. Aaron's priesthood was a type of the future priesthood of Jesus.

A robe was made for Aaron, blue in color (Exod. 28:31), which had a binding around the neck to prevent it from being torn from top to bottom. Around the hem were sown golden bells and a fruit called the "pomegranate." They were placed alternately around the hem of the robe, a bell and a pomegranate so that each pomegranate separated the golden bells, preventing them from clashing together (Exod. 28:33, 34).

The Lord said, "And it shall be on Aaron when he *ministers*; and its tinkling may be heard when he enters and leaves the holy place before the Lord, that he may not die" (Exod. 28:35 NASB).

The golden bells rang while the high priest was in the holy place so the people would know he was *active*, ministering before God on their behalf. When the priest went in and out of the holy place, the people could *hear* the activity of the bells and see the presence of the fruit. If the bells stopped ringing—indicating the high priest had sat down on the job—he would die. Aaron's ministry under the Mosaic law stood prophetically for a more excellent priestly ministry which the Lord would personally provide to His Church.

"But when Christ appeared as a high priest of the good things to come, He entered through the greater and more perfect tabernacle, not made with hands . . . and through His own blood, He entered the holy place once for all, having obtained eternal redemption" (Heb. 9:11-12 NASB).

The high priest who demanded the crucifixion of Jesus "tore his robes" (Matt. 26:65). Such action was strictly forbidden by God (Lev. 21:10). But the high priest was part of the termination of Aaron's priesthood. God confirmed the "rending" of robes worn by carnal "high priests" by tearing the veil of the temple in two from top to bottom when Jesus died on the cross (Matt. 27:50-51).

The high priesthood of God was continuing. The high priesthood of Mosaic law was over. Jesus was now the only high priest God would accept in His presence (Heb. 9:24). He was now the eternal "great priest over the house of God."

Jewish priests didn't understand that God had terminated their work. When the book of Hebrews was written (about 64 A.D.), the Jewish temple was still standing with priests making sacrifices to God. Their work was finally terminated when the Lord permitted the temple to be destroyed in 72 A.D.

The activity of the high priesthood has not changed—only the people and the place. As Jesus moves about actively among His people, the bells on His priestly robe ring. The fruit is present upon His priestly garments. All of this gives the disciple confidence that his High Priest, Jesus Christ, is alive, active and interceding for him in the presence of the Father. Hebrews 2:4

declares that God moved in this way in the early church, confirming the salvation of His people with "signs and wonders and by various miracles and by gifts of the Holy Spirit according to His will" (NASB).

The presence of the gifts of the Spirit (which we hear) and fruit of the Spirit (which we see) confirms the activity of Jesus in our lives, the church and the holy place of God. The gifts and fruit of the Holy Spirit are attached to the holy blue garment which Jesus wears. They are for His "glory and beauty" (Exod. 28:2). The disciple who receives the Spirit of Jesus receives all the gifts and fruit of the Spirit. They are now resident within him.

Releasing Fruit for Ministry

The Spirit-filled disciple, who understands that all nine gifts (1 Cor. 12:7-11) and all nine fruit (Gal. 5:22-23) are resident in his life, is ready for balanced ministry within the body of Christ. The release of the Spirit in his life gives place to the ministry.

The exasperated brother who said, "I just don't seem to have any peace or joy anymore" didn't understand he has an unlimited supply of both *within* himself.

He later told me, "I know I'm supposed to have all that within me but it still doesn't seem to do me any good." The Father has a plan for the disciple which He expects him to follow. In 2 Corinthians 9:10, Paul explained the plan: "He who supplies seed to the sower and bread for food, will supply and multiply your seed for sowing and increase the harvest of your righteousness" (NASB).

The more a person sows God's love, joy and peace, the

more He supplies your needs. The flow of this abundant supply through a disciple's life to others is Christian ministry. You have a greater supply than you need. But you only enjoy it as it flows through your life to others.

"We've got to talk to you," a man announced, walking up to me at the close of a teaching seminar. His wife was a step or two behind. "We're in trouble," he said, gesturing at his lovely wife, who appeared in her early thirties. "We were in love when we got married, but you know how it is after you've been married awhile."

"I know what you're talking about," I agreed. "You look about the ages my wife and I were when we had been married ten years. We were having trouble communicating then."

"But Brother Ligon," the wife spoke up, "we've lost all purpose for continuing this marriage. If it weren't for the children. . . ." Her voice trailed off and her eyes filled with tears.

"My wife is so disappointed in me," the husband said dejectedly. "I'm just not spiritual enough for her. She needs a Billy Graham type for a husband. Then maybe she'd be happy."

"Oh, she could never be happy with anyone but you," I assured the husband. "I want you both to come back tomorrow night. I'm going to teach on the powerful resources available to believers who want to make things work in their lives."

"Boy, is that what we really need," the husband agreed.

The couple was sitting in the front row the next night. They were still disappointed with each other. That was easy to see. But I was confident their marriage could be changed into a honeymoon. It had certainly changed my marriage.

My wife and I had been in the same boat at one time. We had been disappointed with each other. Neither of us could seem to do anything "just right." But God showed us the supernatural power which operates as fruit of the Spirit is released. I now felt like a twenty-one-year-old lover around my wife. At forty, she was lovelier to me than ever.

That night I taught on the principles God had shown me. The unhappy couple sat on the edge of their seats. Afterwards I returned home, forgetting about the situation.

"You missed quite a phone call today," the church secretary announced several weeks later. "You ought to stay around the office more."

"Who was it?" I asked.

"Some housewife from Mississippi," she answered with a smile. "I'm glad she was paying the bill and not me—she talked fifteen minutes."

"Well, what did she have to say?" I questioned, becoming more interested all the time.

"She kept talking about releasing fruit of the Spirit in her life," the secretary answered, brushing a sprig of hair back with her hand. "She thought she'd lost all love for her husband. He never seemed to do anything right. Then, she heard you teaching that all the fruit she ever needed was *inside* her. She decided to start releasing it toward her husband and children. She said her home has changed completely. She and her husband are having the time of their lives. They're on a second honeymoon. She was just calling to thank you."

The renewed couple had learned a great lesson in

discipleship. They had attended seminars and conferences. They had talked to pastors and teachers—all looking for a solution to their problems. Then they discovered the best help they could obtain was within them.

Paul said, "But earnestly desire the greater gifts. And I show you a still more excellent way" (1 Cor. 12:31 NASB). People shift from one extreme to another interpreting this verse. Some only emphasize the gifts of the Spirit, like the church at Corinth. Others deny the ministry of gifts, holding only to the fruit. But Paul said the "more excellent way" was a combination of them. The bells and fruit on the priestly garment of Aaron serve as an example of how fruit and gifts accompany each other in the ministry of Jesus.

A woman who had hemorrhaged for twelve years managed to touch that hem (Mark 5:25-30) and she was healed. What she did caused a release of the power (*dunamin*) of Jesus in her body. She came into contact with the supernatural power of Jesus as His love was released in her.

This woman experienced what Jesus wanted all His disciples to know when He said, "You did not choose Me, but I chose you, and appointed you, that you should go and bear fruit, and that your fruit should remain, that whatever you ask of the Father in My name, He may give to you" (John 15:16 NASB).

Fruit for Ministering

Paul listed nine fruit in Galatians 5:22-23 which are resident in the Holy Spirit—love, joy, peace, patience (longsuffering), kindness (gentleness), goodness, faithfulness, meekness (gentleness) and temperance (self-control).

The fruit, like gifts, fall naturally into three groups of three. The first group—love, joy, peace—are basic spiritual qualities in every disciple's life. They are essential in his own personal character and in his ministry to others.

The second group—patience, kindness, goodness—fit naturally into a disciple's relationship to others. The third group—faithfulness, meekness, temperance—develop a disciple's relationship to God.

Love, Joy and Peace

Love, joy and peace are an extension of the life and personality of the Lord.

"Love suffereth long," "love is patient," "love is kind," Paul said in 1 Corinthians 13:4. The various expressions of fruit are interwoven or interlocked like the joining of grapes in a cluster. The whole of the cluster makes maturity in the disciple an attainable goal.

Love as fruit is the Greek word *agape*. The Bible says that God is love (*agape*). Some people think that love is God, so they pursue love and never find it.

Couples look for love and never find it. People go to church looking for love, then leave criticizing people because they didn't find it. No one has ever found love by looking for it. The Bible says, "But God showed His love (agape) toward us, in that while we were yet sinners, Christ died for us" (Rom. 5:8 NASB).

There are four words in Greek which describe various expressions of love. *Eros* is the first kind. The word "erotic" comes from it, expressing strong personal feelings experienced for another person or thing. Erotic love appears to be noble so long as the object being loved is satisfying.

It is dependent upon the innate quality and beauty of the object. When that quality is lost, the strength of erotic love dies. Many American marriages have been constructed on this kind of love. It's also why America has experienced a skyrocketing divorce rate.

A second word is *philia*. The city of Philadelphia is a composite of two Greek words—*adelphos*, which means brother, and *philia*, which means a friendship-type love. Philadelphia is said to be the city of "brotherly love." There is more nobility in this kind of love. Jesus said, "You are My friends (*philos*), if you do what I command you" (John 15:14 NASB).

The third kind of love is *storge*. This is the love expressed among members of a close family. It is strong among many ethnic families of lesser industrialized countries. This love can be found at times among criminal families who assault outsiders but protect each other with a sacrificial devotion.

Agape love proceeds from the heart of God. It comes from the person of Jesus, the true vine, and flows into His followers, the branches. *Agape* love is manifested as the disciple abides in Jesus. It has the power to love the unlovely, touch the leper, suffer crucifixion at the hands of people, and still desire the highest and best for them.

It is not dependent upon the beauty or value of the other person. It is totally self-motivated. It is able to create value where there is none and restore beauty even though scarred by sin. With it, a gentle and kind man from Nazareth brought an entire Kingdom into submission to

Him. It resides in the disciple and can be released to change the world.

The second fruit, joy, or *chara* in Greek, is the evangelistic tool of the Holy Spirit. It causes the Church to witness and penetrate a lost world for Jesus.

I tried for many years as a Baptist pastor to encourage people to witness. Then to my amazement, I found people filled with the Holy Spirit saying they'd burst if they couldn't tell somebody about Jesus. It's the joy in a believer that makes him talk about Jesus. He just can't keep his mouth shut. Church leaders shouldn't try to stop that. The Holy Spirit used this fruit in disciples' lives at Pentecost to convert 3,000 in one day.

Paul takes special note of this in 1 Thessalonians 1:6-8. "And ye became followers of us, and the Lord, having received the word in much affliction, with *joy* of the Holy Ghost:

"So that ye were *ensamples* to all that believe in Macedonia and Achaia. For from you sounded out the word of the Lord not only in Macedonia and Achaia, but also in every place your faith to God-ward is spread abroad; so that we need not to speak any thing" (italics mine).

Jesus meant for His followers to penetrate the world in just that way. When disciples learn how to release the fruit of joy, Christianity becomes fun. I call this fruit the "trumpet" of the Holy Spirit. When the joy is released, the disciple's mouth flies open and everybody hears about Jesus. He "trumpets" it abroad.

Without the manifestation of joy, the disciple will drift back into his old self-centered ways. He will become burdened with unnecessary problems and rekindle the old energies of his flesh. You don't see a person witnessing about Jesus much when he's preoccupied with his own life.

The fruit of joy keeps the disciple on the witnessing side of evangelism. He cannot keep his mouth shut when the joy arises. It is like the economy-minded housewife who shares her "new find" of a specially priced purchase with her neighbor. The department store didn't hire her for their advertising campaign. In her enthusiasm, she just naturally told about her purchase and where she got it. So it is with the fruit of joy. When you understand what you have in Jesus each day, joy begins to rise up out of you. It naturally results in witnessing and evangelism.

When the body of Christ permits new rules and regulations to control and limit this witness, the seeds of her own decay are sown.

Dr. Elton Trueblood says in *The Company of the Committed*, "If the enkindling fire (Luke 12:49) which Christ said He came to light has in any sense entered his soul, he cannot rest until he lights as many other fires as possible."[1]

The fruit of peace, or *eirene*, gives a disciple confidence. The writer of Hebrews notes the value of confidence. It has "great recompence of reward" (Heb. 10:35). In John 14:27 Jesus talked about this fruit.

"Peace I leave with you; My peace I give to you; not as the world gives, do I give to you. Let not your heart be troubled, nor let it be fearful" (NASB).

A disciple who resists this confidence-producing fruit in his life will become fearful and afraid. This fruit will allow him to relax in the Lord and move forward confidently in Him. Anxiety, tension and fear cannot rule the life of a disciple who is at peace with God. This fruit of peace

[1]Elton Trueblood, *The Company of the Committed*, (New York: Harper & Row, 1961) p. 55.

brings a sense of well-being and total reliance upon the Lord.

Patience, Kindness and Goodness

These fruit—patience, kindness and goodness—equip the disciple to minister to others.

Patience or longsuffering (*makrothumia*) gives the disciple power to remain steadfast in the face of strong provocation or testing. *The Interpreter's Dictionary of the Bible* points out that "the meaning would seem to be that the child of God is to reflect God's attitude of forebearance toward wrongdoers, not condoning evil but hoping that patience will lead him to a better mind."

It is the complaining, criticizing spirit that gets cut off from the blessings of God. Paul and Silas could have easily short-circuited the flow of God's power when they were thrown into the Philippian jail. They could have bellyached and complained—but they didn't. They kept their hearts right and praised God.

God proved to Paul and Silas that there is supernatural power released within this fruit. As the two apostles prayed and sang praises to God their long-suffering grace brought the power of God down upon the jailhouse. The building shook. The chains fell off. The jailer was converted.

Patience has tremendous power. In many situations its release means the difference between answered and unanswered prayers. Disciples who don't flow in this fruit usually give up before God answers.

Gentleness or kindness (*chrestotes*) is the fruit which gives the disciple a loving and sweet disposition. It is a strong weapon against the world's hostilities, releasing strength in the disciple which causes him to be calm and relaxed when others are angry. He has strength to resist a "divisive" spirit which Paul told Titus to reject in believers (Titus 3:10).

The disciple who learns to release this fruit in his life is a valuable asset to any fellowship of believers. His presence unifies, encouraging weaker disciples to be faithful to the work of the Lord.

Many times in counseling situations, I've talked with people who didn't need a trained counselor to minister to them. They only needed this fruit to be released upon them. I have frequently seen brokenhearted people healed as the power of this fruit touches their lives.

Goodness (*agathosune*) is a fruit of the Spirit which gives the disciple power to enjoy his Christian experience.

"I feel so guilty," a young man told me one day. "I was raised in church to serve the Lord. Yet many times I'd like to stay home on Sunday or do something else. I can't do anything else, though, because I've got this fear driving me to be a *good* Christian. Since I'm in church all the time, I wish I could enjoy it."

That same attitude lives with more Christians than they're willing to admit. The body of Christ is filled with believers who haven't learned to achieve a balance in their Christian walk.

Have you ever felt envy for a brother or sister who seemed to get such a "big charge" out of being in church? The fruit of goodness has changed their "have to" to "want to." It releases a gentle and considerate disposition towards others in the body of Christ. Serving Christ takes on an entirely new picture when this fruit is loosed.

Faithfulness, Meekness and Temperance

This cluster of fruit releases the grace within a disciple to relate maturely to the Heavenly Father. These fruit have the supernatural power to turn a rebellious person into a trustworthy bondservant of Jesus Christ.

Faithfulness (*pistis*) is the same word as faith. It is translated as faithfulness in this grouping of fruit.

Faith that is not faithful is only temporary. Without the release of this fruit, a disciple will be a man of faith and power one day and distraught and troubled the next. He can't be completely trusted because his faith response to God is controlled by his circumstances. If he can't change his circumstances rapidly in his favor, he grows fainthearted and slips into doubt.

When faithfulness is released in his life, he becomes honest, trustworthy and reliable in all circumstances. The wise pastor will look for disciples with this fruit flowing. Such a disciple is leadership material. He will be around serving God when most everybody else has fled in the face of difficulty.

Most people try to decide if they can trust God. This disciple convinces God that He can trust him! That's real faithfulness.

Meekness (*praotes*) is a fruit which has often been confused with weakness. That is not the case, however. The best example is the life of Jesus. He was a meek person—but he was not weak. Note the following example about the Lord Jesus.

When the high priest was questioning Jesus (John 18:19-23), an officer "gave Jesus a blow." Jesus answered him, "If I have spoken wrongly, bear witness of the wrong; but if rightly, why do you strike Me?" (verse 23 NASB). Another time He cleansed the temple of money changers, showing He possessed strength. It was that same strength which allowed Him to submit obediently to crucifixion.

This fruit releases the power of God to bring an arrogant and self-assertive spirit into submission to the Lord. It sets him apart as a genuine disciple of Christ—constantly willing to be taught by the Master. Power flows through this fruit for the disciple to mature in all Christian graces.

Temperance or self-control (*egkrateia*) releases wisdom in a disciple's daily walk in the Spirit. Such wisdom could be called "common sense." Many believers are deficient in this fruit. Its release gives power to bring the disciple's own appetites under control.

Many disciples get backed into difficult situations by failing to exercise this fruit. It has the power to bring personal finances under control, reduce self-indulging appetites and keep a wanderer at home. It is the fruit that convinces the outside world there is something good about the Christian life.

Release—An Act of Obedience

The difference between success and failure often depends on a disciple's willingness to release what God has already put *within* him. That truth had never been more clearly demonstrated to me than on a trip my wife and I made teaching in a seminar in a small mountain town in north Georgia.

A middle-aged businessman who had been a Christian for many years came to the meetings and was stirred by the Holy Spirit. He had lived a decent life growing up in a full-gospel church—but he had never received the gift of tongues. By talking with the man, I believed he was genuinely born again. And since he had already asked for the Holy Spirit, I also believed he had the gift *within* him. He didn't understand that God gives the Holy Spirit "to those who ask Him" (Luke 11:13).

On the seminar's final night, I called him forward. "Glenn, do you believe God can do anything he wants?" I asked.

"Oh, sure, sure," he answered, almost fearful to question the Almighty's great power.

"Okay, then do you believe you can speak and the Holy Spirit will take those utterances and turn them into a language?"

"Yeah, he can do anything he wants to," he allowed.

"Okay, then how did you learn to speak English?"

"By just making sounds."

"Right. Now you've begged God many times to give you this gift since you were a child. I'm going to begin praying to the Lord. When I feel I should, I'll start praying in the Spirit. At that time, I want you to pray in anything but English."

I started praying and Glenn, reluctantly but obediently, followed behind. "Da, da, de, de," he mumbled along.

Before long his "da, da's and de, de's" had turned into "gu, gu's." Then I heard him repeat, "Gloria a Dios." Before long, he was praising God in the most beautiful Spanish I had ever heard.

"Glenn, what have you been saying?" I asked.

"I don't know," he answered, wiping away the tears. "It

sounded like gibberish to me but it sure made me feel good.”

“Well, I just want you to know that I’m bilingual and I speak Spanish. You were praising God in perfect Spanish.”

“Praise God,” he shouted jubilantly. “I had it all the time and didn’t know it.”

For the first time in his life, Glenn recognized this significant truth from God. The gift had been there all the time.

If a believer has the Holy Spirit, every gift and fruit of the Holy Spirit is resident. It is impossible to dissect the personality of God, separating one part of Him from another. God is God. He is the great I AM. When He resides in a human life, He resides in the fullness of His personality.

12 | *Six Faulty Foundations*

Extremist's seeds were sown widely in the nineteenth century. It was a time in Church history noted for captivating leaders who led away disciples by emphasizing one extreme belief.

Frederick A. Norwood in *The Development of Modern Christianity Since 1500* gives an example of how the application of "methods" to one extreme started an entire new movement. Norwood writes:

"Mrs. Mary Baker Eddy, after years of affliction, physical and mental, found relief through a mental healer in Portland, Maine. Adapting and reorienting the method, Mrs. Eddy wrote and published in 1875 a textbook, *Science and Health*. This set forth the basic principles of Christian Science, centered around the denial or nonexistence of matter, evil, sin, and death. From this teaching came a new religion, using but not relying on the Bible, the Church of Christ, Scientist. Its major appeal was faith healing."[1]

[1]Frederick A. Norwood, *The Development of Modern Christianity Since 1500*, (New York: Abingdon Press, 1956), p. 176.

It was misuse of the Bible which led Mrs. Eddy into extremism. She apparently read into the Scriptures what she wanted them to say.

Paul said to the Corinthians, "As a wise masterbuilder, I laid a foundation. . . . For no man can lay a foundation other than the one which is laid, which is Jesus Christ" (1 Cor. 3:10-11).

The wise disciple will be careful to avoid certain extremes as he "builds the foundation." Tragedies occur in life. The greatest tragedy would be to discover on Judgment Day that a serious disciple had built on the wrong foundation. At the risk of overlooking some, I suggest six faulty foundations to help the disciple recognize and avoid them.

A word of caution is advisable, however, as one begins to look for extremes in the teachings of others. No extreme has injured more in the body of Christ than that of calling another man's work "satanic" when his doctrine disagrees with your own. For hundreds of years, this unchristian method has been used to label sincere believers as heretics.

James wrote that the tongue is a "restless evil and full of deadly poison. With it we bless our Lord and Father; and with it we curse men, who have been made in the likeness of God" (James 3:8-9 NASB).

The tactic was first employed when the Pharisees accused the work of Jesus as being satanic. It has been greatly overworked ever since.

No admonition has been as gracious and wise as the one found in James 5:19-20, "My brethren, if any among you strays from the truth, and one turns him back, let him know that he who turns a sinner from the error of his way will save his soul from death, and will cover a multitude of sins" (NASB).

The work of men rises and falls as they come into various degrees of truth—but the Lord is forever. The greatest truth we can expound is unity in the body of Christ with Jesus at the helm.

If all genuine believers would bend enough to conform to His ways, the church could make great strides toward restoration today. Then, anyone who moved away from truth into any degree of error would find a company of committed believers encouraging him back into balance. Fellowship in the family could then be restored.

By-passing the Head of the Church

Paul said, "Let no one keep defrauding you of your prize by . . . not holding fast to the Head, from whom the entire body, being supplied and held together by the joints and ligaments, grows with a growth which is from God" (Col. 2:18-19 NASB).

A disciple who puts blind trust in a reputable church leader will find it hard to detect error in the teacher. Yet no man is infallible. Respect for anointed leaders is scriptural (Heb. 13:17). However, the teacher who doesn't recognize the possibility of error creeping into his life is a proud man. Shepherds who disciple believers to Jesus Christ must always hold Jesus up between themselves and their pupils.

When Paul realized certain brothers were relying upon the teacher more than the Lord, he wrote, "We are God's fellow-workers; you are God's field, God's building" (1 Cor. 3:9). Paul knew better than to get between God and man. He had done that as a Pharisee, choosing to exercise judgment over the people of God. The burning power of God shook him of that notion on the Damascus Road.

A teaching was given recently throughout charismatic circles that graphically illustrates the way men can move away from the Head of the Church in their Bible teachings. In John, chapter 10, Jesus used the allegory of a sheepfold to show how He and He alone is the door to the sheep. He indicated in verse nine that He is the door and those who go in find both salvation and pasture.

Verses one through five are an allegory. This is clear in verse six where John states that this *paroimia* (allegory) He spoke to them. Verse six indicates that they (the Pharisees) didn't understand what Jesus was saying so He repeated the allegory more specifically.

Jesus repeated that He was the door to the sheep. He didn't mention any other door. The sheep come in through that door (verse nine) and are saved (*sothesetai*)—they are safe and sound. In verse 11, He identified himself as the good Shepherd. In verse 12, He's identified as the Owner. In verses 14 and 16, He knows His sheep by name, they hear His voice and they all become *one* flock with *one* shepherd. That is the message of the allegory.

There have been teachings which use these verses but which say that since Jesus was the Shepherd and the pastor was "a shepherd," then the pastor was "a door" just as Jesus was the Door. The only way a person could get to the sheep was to go through the shepherd.

"The door to any flock is the shepherd," stated one Bible teacher quoting John 10:7 as reference. Yet that verse specifically quotes Jesus as saying, "I am the door of the sheep."

That same Bible teacher also said that the life flows

through relationships, using 1 John 1:1-7 as his basis. That Scripture actually supports the position that all fellowship is "with the Father and with His Son, Jesus Christ" (1 John 1:3 NASB).

It is obvious in both these Scriptures that the Lord was describing a unilateral relationship of each member within the body to Jesus Christ while showing in 1 John 1:3 that we also have fellowship with each other.

Yet the Bible teacher further compared relationships in the body of Christ to the members of a man's body. He stated that since members of his physical body were not joined directly to his head but to their members in particular, Christ's body was the same way. He taught that the reason we know we're joined to the Head, Jesus Christ, is that we are joined to another member. He then encouraged those listening not to join a body, but to join a shepherd.

According to the teacher, the shepherd would be responsible for the disciple. He would protect, train and love him. No doubt there is *some* truth in everything the teacher said.

But the Lord Jesus Christ was teaching a salvation principle in John 10. He taught that there was only one Door into the sheepfold (the Church) and He was that door.

The Bible teacher in question apparently decided where he was going before he selected the Scripture. He then bent it to fit into his study plan. He was obviously trying to guide his audience in a preplanned direction.

Scholars call that method "eisegesis." That is, the teacher reads into the text of Scripture what he wants it to say. Thousands of trusting disciples have been led into error throughout Church history by just such handling of Holy Scripture.

Invading Sovereign Authority

The second area of faulty foundations is that of invading sovereign authority. That is, a person moves into areas of authority which the Bible reserves solely for God the Father, God the Son, and God the Holy Spirit.

Throughout the ages, men and women alike have been called upon to blindly trust those who have spiritual authority over them in the church. Their trust would be shown by their willingness to submit their wills to their leaders. If leaders were in error, the trusting disciples were supposed to leave it up to God to correct them.

Respect for church leaders who had only delegated authority was considered a "shallow" commitment by some. Disciples were called upon to submit their lives to a pastor or shepherd "as unto the Lord" for the purpose of forming mature character.

Insecure pastors and shepherds who did not know how to accept such bold authority over people's lives have led many into devastating situations. Some wounds were hard to heal. Others never recovered.

It has been difficult for men to understand that God alone exercises authority over the conscience of another. Reformers wrote safeguards into their confessions of faith to instruct their members about such violations.

The Westminster Confession of Faith is a case in point. Its writers clearly defined the necessity of all believers reserving their conscience for the Sovereign God to probe. Paul declared that he worked with a clear conscience before God.

Martin Luther took his stand before the assembly in the first Diet at Worms on the authority of Holy Scriptures and the integrity of his conscience. When called upon to recant and place himself in absolute submission to the Pope he responded, "Unless I am refuted and convicted by testimonies of the Scriptures or by clear arguments . . . I cannot and will not recant anything, since *it is unsafe and dangerous to do anything against the conscience.*"[2]

In the early nineteenth century, William R. Williams, a lawyer and minister from New York state, wrote an eloquent defense for the conscience of man, in which he called for communities of men not to ask for any "transfer of conscience."

Jeremiah said, " 'Behold, days are coming,' declares the Lord, 'when I will make a new covenant with the house of Israel and with the house of Judah, not like the covenant which I made with their fathers. . . . But this is the covenant which I will make with the house of Israel after those days,' declares the Lord, 'I will put My law within them, and on their heart I will write it; and I will be their God, and they shall be my people.

" 'And they shall not teach again, each man his neighbor and each man his brother, saying "Know the Lord," for they shall all know Me, from the least of them to the greatest of them,' declares the Lord, 'for I will forgive their iniquity, and their sin I will remember no more' " (Jer. 31:31-34 NASB).

Each man would be responsible for his own sins, according to Jeremiah. No man could assume responsibility for another man. Not only is that a biblical truth, it is also a judicial truth.

[2]Qualben, op. cit., pp. 236-237.

The Nuremberg Trials of 1945 confirmed again a man's responsibility for his own actions. Even though Nazi war criminals came to trial saying they "only did what they were told," the international tribunal ruled otherwise. The tribunal said a man is responsible for his own actions—even during a time of war.

Denying the Authority of Scripture

Reformers from the time of the twelfth-century Waldensians have declared the Holy Scriptures as the final authority for faith and order in the church.

In John 5:39, Jesus told the Pharisees the purpose of Scripture. "You search the Scriptures, because you think that in them you have eternal life; and it is these that bear witness of Me" (NASB).

Luke noted another purpose for Scripture in Acts 17:11. According to the text, the Jews at Berea were more noble-minded than those at Thessalonica, "for they received the word with great eagerness, examining the Scriptures daily, to see whether these things were so" (NASB). They were checking on the teachings of Paul and Silas. I get the impression some believers would be afraid to do that today.

When leaders down through Church history moved away from using the Scriptures as the final authority for faith and order, three patterns developed bringing decay with them.

First, church leaders began teaching that members of the body of Christ were too ignorant to understand the Bible for themselves. The Lord's sheep were considered to be dumb! They had to be told what to do. Understanding Holy Scripture was considered only possible at higher echelons of ministry. Therefore, the sheep had to be "properly" connected in order to receive revelation from the Bible.

Unquestionably, sheep are dumb—but human beings aren't. Human beings are qualified to be the temple of God. Sheep are not. The Holy Spirit can fill people and teach them the ways of God. Disciples with a hunger for the Word can hear from God as quickly as shepherds. That may be "earth-shaking" news to some shepherds but it is an established fact.

Second, tradition began taking precedence over the canon of Holy Scriptures. Disciples became preoccupied with what the shepherds *said* the Word of God said. When that trend runs full course, it becomes tradition.

Third, prophecies began being received as having equal authority as the Word of God. The Church of Jesus Christ of Latter Day Saints (Mormons) began in 1815 in just that way.

Kenneth Scott Latourette in *A History of Christianity* states, "Its founder, Joseph Smith . . . believed that he had visions which told him that no existing ecclesiastical body represented the divine will and that God had chosen him to restore the true church. He maintained that at the behest of the visions he dug in a hill, found a book written in strange characters, and translated it through miraculous assistance."[3]

That translation, published in 1830, was included in the *Book of Mormon*. The source of doctrine for the entire Mormon church became the *Book of Mormon* and the *Bible*. The so-called prophecy had gained equal authority with the Word of God.

Many believers blindly accept the teachings of certain

[3]Kenneth Scott Latourette, *A History of Christianity*, (New York: Harper & Row, 1953), p. 1233.

Bible teachers, not realizing that God has established sole authority in the Holy Scriptures. If a Bible teacher—regardless of his position or prominence—departs from a balanced presentation of the Scriptures, the Word of God is still the final authority.

Adding to or taking from the Scriptures is strictly "off limits" to the disciple of Christ (Rev. 22:18-19). The Bible has demonstrated again and again that it is God's anointed written Word to guide men successfully through this earthly life and around the pitfalls of error.

Attempting to protect their disciples from error, men have always tried to control the Bible teachings their followers received. Yet Paul said, "there must also be factions (heresies) among you, in order that those who are approved may have become evident among you" (1 Cor. 11:19 NASB). According to Paul, the Holy Spirit actually permitted the believer to be exposed to error so he would be strengthened by the truth which is in him and in the Word.

The disciple actually matures in Christ as he learns to compare the teachings of various men with the Word of God. Only man—in the name of responsible pastoral leadership—would attempt to censor everything a disciple receives. If man can control a disciple's diet, he can control his very life.

Disregarding the Priesthood of All Believers

Peter said, "You also, as living stones, are being built up as a spiritual house for a holy *priesthood*, to offer up spiritual sacrifices acceptable to God through Jesus Christ" (1 Peter 2:5 NASB, italics mine). "But you are a chosen race," he continued in verse nine, "a royal priesthood, a holy nation, a people for God's own possession. . . ."

In two sweeping statements, Peter had located every new Christian in a family of priests in which each member functioned as a priest.

The disciples who had known worship in Judaism had seen only a select group of men from a single tribe functioning as priests. But in the kingdom of God, participation in all priestly functions under the High Priesthood of Jesus Christ was considered basic. Newborn babes were immediately introduced into a functioning royal priesthood (*basileion hierateuma*).

In this "holy nation" each member was plugged into Jesus Christ. He was expected to receive all the necessary life flow of the Kingdom from Him. Each member was also to offer worship to God and make known His goodness to the world.

Teachings which removed the disciple from this privileged position with Jesus Christ have been introduced into the body of Christ in recent years. The teachings placed intermediaries in a priestly role between the believer and Jesus.

Built upon the "vine" and "branch" metaphor used by Jesus in John 15, the teachings attempted to show disciples how to produce good fruit in their lives. Yet extreme doctrine was introduced when the metaphor was developed beyond the actual text.

Relationships were shown to be established between smaller branches and more mature branches to which they were connected and from which they received their growth. The more mature men were the first ones to grow from the vine and were directly connected to it. The younger disciples (branches) grew from the older ones and drew the life of Jesus through them.

As sap flowed from the main body of the plant, through the principal branches and out to the smaller ones, life was supposed to flow to all the body of Christ. All of this was to permit the disciple to realize the fullness of the kingdom—righteousness, peace and joy. It was said that such a relationship permitted the disciple to develop Christian maturity through the oversight of his shepherd. Each shepherd, in turn, received his oversight from another shepherd to whom he was submitted.

An examination of John 15 shows that Jesus had each branch (disciple) plugged directly into the vine (the Lord Jesus). "I am the vine," He said. That relationship was described as "abiding" (*menō*). Thus, the branch remained attached to the vine and continually drew life from it.

Each time Jesus referred to this abiding relationship, He used the singular noun for branch (*klēma*). In verse five, Jesus addressed the disciples corporately as branches (*klēmata*). In the next breath when He spoke of "abiding," He returned to a singular pronoun. Any branch not personally joined to the vine and abiding in it would wither and die, according to Jesus (verse six).

Extreme teachings on covenant relationships have also been introduced in the church in the last several years. One such teaching tries to "build" covenant relationships between brothers in Christ—a work Jesus has already completed. Most teaching on the subject overlooks the basis for covenant relationships.

The metaphor of the vine and the branch from John 15

illustrates the scriptural position of covenant relationships. Most scholars agree that life flowing from the vine to each branch is the basis for *koinōnia* fellowship in the body of Christ.

Each branch enjoys the covenant relationship which permits him to draw life from the Lord Jesus. The covenant which permits that relationship is unilateral. God alone determines everything about it—provision for the branches, demands placed upon them, and the behavior of one branch to another.

God guarantees the covenant will work. He seals it with the blood of His Son and insures the relationship with His Holy Name. He gives man free choice to accept or refuse the covenant. If he accepts, he is "born again" into the family of God.

Entering the family of God gives a person brothers and sisters who are already in covenant with him because they're in covenant with the same Father. Recognizing then that they are the family of God, each person must learn to love one another.

Failing to understand the covenant God has already established, recent teachings have used the relationships of David to Jonathan and Paul to Timothy as models for covenants which are supposed to be worked out. When one disciple tries to establish a covenant relationship with another, the conditions of the disciple's priesthood with Jesus are violated. How can they "work out" what had already been worked out for them?

Confusion frequently sets in as the disciple attempts to meet conditions of the covenant with his brother. Unable to achieve the satisfaction he experienced with the Lord Jesus, the disciple often sinks into condemnation and defeat. The relationship becomes a weight for him to bear rather than a freedom to experience.

I have seen this happen in the home between our two sons. They have "squared off" to fight at times, trying to exercise authority over one another. Peace was only restored when they released the authority they were struggling to exercise back to me as their father and then returned to being brothers.

"I enjoy being a father and I want you to enjoy being brothers," I have told them. "I am the father in this house. I'm not trying to be a brother to either of you and I don't want you to try to assume my role as father." Clarification of those roles settled us into fulfilling relationships. It will do the same within the body of Christ.

Abusing Delegated Authority

Delegated authority is that authority transferred to the members of the body of Christ to carry on the work of the Lord. It is clearly defined in the New Testament and does not allow a church leader to invade sovereign control over a disciple's life.

It is strong enough so discipline can be established within the body of Christ, yet broad enough so the individual does not lose his identity. Such authority gives the church freedom to recognize the Holy Spirit's actions as He appoints and anoints disciples to church offices.

Paul says, "And He gave some as apostles, and some as prophets, and some as evangelists, and some as pastors and teachers, for the equipping of the saints for the work of service, to the building up of the body of Christ" (Eph. 4:11-12). The offices of elders and deacons, along with a number of other ministries including the five-fold ministries mentioned above, all operate in the area of delegated authority.

Many problems have developed in the body of Christ due to extremes and abuses in this area. Innocent people have been hurt as unhappy "saints" have acted in haste to judge and remove anointed men of God from office. Their tactics for expulsion would often disgrace the average secular corporation.

After David had been anointed to succeed Saul as king, he could have taken Saul's life but he wisely refused. "Far be it from me because of the Lord that I should do this thing to my lord, the Lord's anointed, to stretch out my hand against him, since he is the Lord's anointed" (1 Sam. 24:6 NASB).

David was a smart man. He knew God could take care of Saul. If David tried to do it, God would deal with him.

The spreading of the gospel has been hindered by churches which refused to recognize the Holy Spirit's work in raising up men into areas of service. Jesus proclaimed, "Therefore beseech the Lord of the harvest to send out workers into His harvest" (Matt. 9:38 NASB).

Insecure leaders have often been afraid to give responsibility to a budding prospect. It can be a threat to some men. Moving to exercise control over the situation, a pastor can be dictatorial in his treatment of God's people. Damaging rifts have occurred when disciples tried to force recognition of their ministries.

Two approaches have been used by men who were either unable or unwilling to recognize various ministries within the body of Christ. First, the pastor has refused to give place to any other authority but his own. Thus, an entire congregation was brought under his control. The second has been for men to move into one-on-one submission, where all men in submitted relationships come under their authority.

A lack of balance has been created within certain churches when elders refused to recognize or respect the five-fold gift ministries. Someone has rightly observed that each time a pastor moves from one church to another the pastor's authority diminishes and the elders' gains. Finally, it reaches the point the pastor becomes a hireling.

With his authority lost, the pastor can no longer follow the Holy Spirit's leadership in his pastoral ministry. He then becomes unable to minister effectively. Such difficult situations have caused pastors to group together for support and protection.

Scripturally, the pastor is part of the five-fold ministries of the church listed in Ephesians 4:11. They operate at times both locally and extra-locally. When a pastor can be hired or fired "at will," his delegated authority from the Lord is severely restricted. Five-fold ministries are anointed by God as gifts to His church. God will respect those who respect His order.

Neglecting the Mission of the Church

Failure to recognize the mission of the Christian Church in its total perspective has been a colossal defect in the body of Christ. For centuries, men have satisfied themselves in guiding the Church in the direction of their own personal interests.

Nowhere is this failure to understand the Church's overall mission better illustrated than in disregard of evangelism. This is one of the most pronounced voids in some areas of the Church.

Extreme teachings have suggested that a shepherd cannot disciple more sheep than Jesus had disciples. Such teachings have shifted pastors' emphasis in one direction—the development of character in their disciples.

Jesus declared, "For the Son of man is come to seek and to save that which was lost" (Luke 19:10 NASB). The Word of God does not state in any Scripture that a man cannot lead more men to Christ than he can effectively disciple. The church grew numerically when men caught the vision of proclaiming Jesus Christ to lost souls.

It was the church at Antioch which sent Paul, Barnabas, Silas and others out to convert the Gentiles. The Christian advance flourished in Europe during the twelfth, thirteenth and fourteenth centuries when monastics caught the vision of converting the heathen to Christ. Their exodus from the world into cloistered communities had deprived society of their Christ-like "salt and light." Finally, the Spirit of God moved upon men's hearts, turning their emphasis outward to evangelize the lost. Thousands of converts were brought to Christ as a result of the change.

Some churches have also lost sight of their overall mission by refusing to permit women to assume any God-ordained responsibilities within the body of Christ. This shortsightedness has caused great damage to women of God.

Outside of their soul salvation, woman is the most precious gift God has given to man. Jesus elevated women to the place of dignity in society. He took great pains to reach them. The Scripture notes that women supported His ministry financially (Luke 8:3).

Paul commended Phoebe, a deaconness of the church of Cenchrea, to the church at Rome (Rom. 16:1). He instructed husbands to love their wives with the same attention and care that they give to their own bodies (Eph. 5:25-29).

Philip, the evangelist, had four daughters who prophesied in the church (Acts 21:9). They worked along with the apostle Paul, Clement and other fellow workers in the "cause of the gospel" (Phil. 4:3). Homes of women were used for believers' meetings (Acts 16:40). Although there is no scriptural evidence that a woman was ever placed in an office of authority over man in any one of the five-fold ministries (Eph. 4:11), opportunities for ministry and service were open to her.

Extremes in submission teachings have eliminated women from serving in ministries alongside their husbands. One husband and wife team—used extensively in a healing and miracle-working ministry—experienced a loss of anointing after they submitted themselves to one shepherd. They subsequently dropped out of public ministry.

Possibly the most divisive extreme within the church centers around the training of leadership. In many denominations, the church has been nothing more than a preaching station. "Dip 'em and drop 'em" has been the theme of many churches. In such places, the church lost sight of its vision as a "community of believers" as well as a "center" for evangelistic outreach.

On the other hand, the shepherdship movement has taken extreme methods of discipline from various reformers in Church history. Rigid methods have been adopted to disciple hundreds of new converts, as well as church members from traditional church backgrounds.

Obedience, incessant and implicit, was Loyola's favorite lesson to his disciples. One shepherdship teacher stated in an article in 1974 that since the purpose of a true disciple was to carry out the will of Jesus Christ, "his own will must be broken."

To do this, the teacher proposed that the disciple learn to obey his leader as a slave, not "knowing the 'why' of it." Then, he said, the day of recognition would come when his leader would tell him, "Now you are ready." A true disciple, he said, could not be promoted or minister beyond "the recognition of his leader."

When he learned such obedience from his leader, he would then hear the Lord say, "No longer do I call you slaves . . . but I have called you friends" (John 15:15). But to get there with Jesus, the disciple had to let his pastor break his will.

It is obvious that when men have not had the answers to the perplexing problems which challenged them, they have resorted to methods of absolute authority in attempting to solve them.

13 | *The Church God Planned*

Two crucial questions face the body of Christ today. "Is it possible for the Church to properly disciple believers to Jesus Christ and evangelize the world at the same time? And, must we abandon the Church for some other form of body ministry?"

Jesus expected the Church (*ekklēsia*) to work. It did in the first century. Innovative men of God filled with the Holy Spirit can discover how He wants it to work now.

Elton Trueblood in *The Company of the Committed* says, "The best way to understand what the church ought to do is to try to understand what the church is. The partially realized or even unrealized dream is our most precious possession because it shows us where we fail and helps us, accordingly, to see the direction in which we ought to be moving."[1]

One resounding truth rings out from the pages of Church history. No discipleship movement has had permanency which has not respected the total mission of

[1] Elton Trueblood, *The Company of the Committed*, (New York: Harper & Row, 1961) p. 91.

the Church as Christ planned it and the Holy Spirit formed it.

Bodies of believers whose influence has survived the past and made effective contributions to the mission of the Church have known some degree of balance between internal discipline and evangelistic outreach. They have respected the concept of Church as a family of God where all—men, women and children—would enjoy the blessings of God and realize their highest for Him.

Even in the monastic movement—where men first sought seclusion from the world—this concept of the total mission of the Church was respected in some religious orders. Those orders, in particular, have succeeded in maintaining greater continuation throughout the ages.

The People God Called

God did not select a nation already in existence and call it to be His chosen people. After Adam rebelled against God and moved into the extreme of self-sufficiency, God moved to create a true people for himself.

That people would be known as a "community." It would be like an ingathering or a great assembly—with the members coming from "all the families of the earth" (Gen. 12:3c).

God began this work of creating a people by starting with an individual, Abraham. "Now the Lord said to Abram, 'Go forth from your country, And from your relatives And from your father's house, To the land which I will show you; And I will make you a great nation" (Gen. 12:1-2a NASB).

The plan was still in effect even though Abraham's sons, Isaac and Jacob, demonstrated they didn't recognize the purpose of God in having a family to be "My people." God then moved on to gather His people in one person—Jesus Christ, the Son of Man.

The nation of Israel had moved into elitism, considering herself "God's chosen" and all others "Gentile dogs." Yet Jesus Christ came to extend the "call of God" to all men (Eph. 2:12-16).

Paradoxically, Jesus Christ was both "individual"— "abolishing in His flesh" man's sin against God—and also "community"—gathering in himself a people from all nations to make them into "one new man" (Eph. 2:15).

Not long after Jesus completed the Sermon on the Mount, He told His disciples, "And I say to you, that many shall come from east and west, and recline at table with Abraham, and Isaac, and Jacob, in the kingdom of heaven" (Matt. 8:11 NASB). The ingathering was clear in God's mind. His plan to gather His people had never actually changed.

Paul saw the consistency in God's plan, saying, "For neither is circumcision anything, nor uncircumcision, but a new creation. And those who will walk by this rule, peace and mercy be upon them and upon the Israel of God" (Gal. 6:15-16 NASB).

The Israel of God was a new creation. Paul confirmed this when he wrote, "But it is not as though the word of God has failed. For they are not all Israel who are descended from Israel, neither are they all children because they are Abraham's descendants. . . . but the children of the promise are regarded as descendants" (Rom. 9:6-8 NASB).

The church (*ekklēsia*) in the New Testament then was a

fulfillment of the old, fulfilled in Jesus Christ, and an expression of the new, an ingathering of believers in Him. This holy nation would be the people of God, "the called out ones." The Church God planned.

The Church as Jesus Ordained It

The smallest unit of the Church as Jesus saw it was two or three believers assembled in one place (Matt. 18:20). The divine mystery making that possible was embodied in His own Person. Jesus was committed to be present when they "gathered together" in His name. His presence as Head of the corporate body of believers completed the Church. Without Him, the Church didn't exist—no matter how many were present.

Various theologians have suggested since the word "church" or *ekklesia* appears only twice in the Bible (Matt. 16:18, 18:17), Jesus did not intend to establish the Church as the Holy Spirit later formed it. That kind of theology overlooks one gigantic fact. God is always consistent with himself.

It was God the Father who planned the Church as a people of God. It was God the Son who broke into human history to gather the people of God. It was God the Holy Spirit who formed the Church in a group of believers at Pentecost.

When Jesus Christ arrived, God was making a personal call on earth to create His people in Israel. "For out of you shall come forth a Ruler, Who will shepherd My people Israel" (Matt. 2:6 NASB).

Jesus walked among the people of Israel ministering at three levels of community life. He first ministered to the masses (Matt. 4:17, 5:1). The other synoptic writers agree (Mark 1:14, Luke 4:14-16). It was while Jesus was preaching to the masses that the first disciples responded and committed themselves to Him (Matt. 4:18-20).

He continued in public ministry, gathering other disciples and training the original twelve. Finally, he took three disciples aside to witness His transfiguration. His concept of working with two or three was reinforced by His words, "Where two or three have gathered together in my name, there I am in their midst" (Matt. 18:20 NASB).

Jesus functioned effectively in small-group relationships, in the training of leadership and in mass evangelism—all at the same time. His disciples saw the balance in such a ministry. It was easier, then, for them to flow into that balance when the New Testament church was begun at Pentecost. In spite of their human prejudices and worldly hangups, the disciples were able to let the Holy Spirit form the Church as He wanted it.

The Church as the Holy Spirit Formed It

The local assembly of believers at Jerusalem was the first manifestation of the body of Christ. Interestingly, the Holy Spirit didn't move on people in other cities at the same time. It was at Jerusalem first.

The first local church was the laboratory where new disciples experienced the transforming power of God's Word. Three thousand new converts came in one day. Jesus had only trained twelve men to minister to the people. If they had tried to break the number down equally among themselves, that gave each disciple over 250 people.

The number increased again shortly (Acts 4:4). Then "multitudes" of men and women were added (Acts 5:14). Even in the middle of such growth, the believers found time to devote themselves to the apostles' teaching (Acts 2:42).

They maintained the fellowship (*koinōnia*), breaking bread together, holding prayer meetings, and staying in one mind with "gladness and sincerity of heart" (Acts 2:46). Only the Spirit of God moving supernaturally in a community of believers could do that!

The structure was soon expanded to accommodate the growing body. According to Acts 2:46, they related to each other in the general assembly (temple) and in small groups (from house to house). They next selected "seven men of good reputation, full of the Spirit and wisdom" (Acts 6:3 NASB) to take charge of the daily serving of food to widows who were being overlooked.

Then some of the seven felt the anointing of the Holy Spirit for ministries that expanded the body of Christ to other towns and regions. Stephen, one of the seven, boldly preached the word in Jerusalem. Great signs and wonders were seen among the people as he preached (Acts 6:8).

As persecution of the church increased, Philip moved to Samaria where his preaching drew many to believe on Jesus (Acts 8:5-7). The Holy Spirit had confirmed him in the ministry of evangelism, one of the five-fold of the church (Eph. 4:11).

It was the evangelistic ministry at work which opened the doors for the apostolic (Acts 4:14), pastoral and teaching ministries (Acts 11:26) to be dispatched from Jerusalem to Antioch for laying the right foundation to the new church. The prophet Agabus also came from Jerusalem and ministered in Antioch.

The latter's arrival completed the sending of all five-fold ministries—apostles, prophets, evangelists, pastors, teachers—in their job of "equipping [of] the saints for the work of service, to the building up of the body of Christ" (Eph. 4:12 NASB).

The five-fold ministers did their work well in Antioch. They had prayed with the new believers, laying hands on them to be filled with the Holy Spirit. Barnabas came from Jerusalem to pastor the congregation the first year with Paul's help, teaching "considerable numbers."

It was from Antioch that the cycle began all over again. The cycle—evangelistic outreach, confirmation of new disciples, laying a good foundation, setting elders to oversee the work, ministering through the five-fold offices—gave balance to other new works.

The Holy Spirit has consistently carried out the work according to the plan of God. Scriptural evidence confirms the fact that God expects the Holy Spirit to continue His mission of forming the body of Christ until Jesus returns.

Paul declared in Philippians 1:6, "For I am confident of this very thing, that He who began a good work in you will perfect it until the day of Christ Jesus" (NASB). Paul trusted the Holy Spirit to complete His work in the life of each disciple.

Each generation of believers has had to face the question, "Can the Holy Spirit be trusted in the formation of the Church of Jesus Christ?"

Yet is there any reason to believe God would change His methods of church development in midstream? Do men today have access to "new revelation" from God which previous generations have not had?

The answer is a resounding "no" to both questions.

Each generation has had the same opportunity to receive the full revelation of God through a personal encounter with Jesus Christ, the risen Lord. Such an unveiling of God will come to the disciple as "fresh" revelation—it is there that God speaks.

"That which has been is that which will be,
And that which has been done is that which will be done.
So, there is nothing new under the sun.
Is there anything of which one might say,
'See this, it is new'?
Already it has existed for ages
Which were before us.
There is no remembrance of earlier things;
And also of the later things which will occur,
There will be for them no remembrance
Among those who will come later still."
(Eccles. 1:9-11 NASB)

14 | *Foundations for Tomorrow's Church*

What will keep the church of tomorrow from becoming as cold and institutionalized as it was by the second century? How can the body of Christ recognize extremes and maintain balance?

The problems are as old as Christendom. And the simple truth is that we don't have the power to prevent them.

Efforts on the part of zealous men to build lasting safeguards against heresy in the Church have also led to extremes. Paul noted, "For there must also be factions (heresies) among you, in order that those who are approved may have become evident among you" (1 Cor. 11:19 NASB).

It has always rested in the hands of each succeeding generation to study the Word of God, stay close to Jesus and follow the direction of the Holy Spirit.

Some generations have handled it better than others. A few have been so weak that God has had to move in new and sovereign ways to restore spiritual vitality to the church. Still others have passed on great character and faith to their children.

Church leaders who tried to guarantee balance by establishing rigid controls over the sheep have not succeeded. The better approach would be for leaders to define their faith for all to understand. Psalm 127:1 exhorts, "Unless the Lord builds the house, they labor in vain who build it" (NASB).

The best contribution that can be made to tomorrow's church is for each disciple to understand his own day and be faithful to it—as David did. It is up to each believer to "fully carry out the preaching of the Word of God, that is, the mystery which has been hidden from the past ages and generations; but has now been manifested to His saints, to whom God willed to make known what is the riches of the glory of this mystery among the Gentiles, which is Christ in you, the hope of glory" (Col. 1:25-27 NASB).

Understanding Foundation Guidelines

The apostle Paul wisely stated, "According to the grace of God which was given to me, as a wise masterbuilder I laid a foundation, and another is building upon it. But let each man he careful how he builds upon it" (1 Cor. 3:10 NASB).

The Bible offers certain guidelines which will help a body of believers stay in balance. One brother remarked, "Some people have to run into the ditch before they learn where the middle of the road is." Running into ditches, however, can injure people. Formation of good driving habits and understanding the rules of the road help drivers remain in the center and out of ditches. The same is true for church leaders. They can avoid extremes by adopting proper guidelines and shunning bad habits.

The twentieth century is a rapidly developing technological age. Demands are heavy upon church leaders to discern the mentality of the time and rise to meet the challenge.

It has been suggested that the current secular, industrial age offers the greatest challenge. Yet I believe no challenge to the Church was any greater than that which faced the first-century Christians from persecution.

The apostles had no precedence for laying their foundations. Their doctrinal background was the tradition of the scribes and Pharisees. They had to take Jesus Christ as their example and live by every word He taught them. They had to learn to rely upon the Holy Spirit.

In contrast, the Church today has nearly 2,000 years of trial and error behind it. Church historians have diligently recorded those 2,000 years of experience for the believers' benefit. A search of Church history reflects that problems in discipleship extremes have been repeated in each generation.

Competition in demanding men's religious loyalty was great during the first century of Christianity. Rome, then an occupying state, supported its own gods and demanded worship of the emperor as the first allegiance. Politics and heathen worship were interwoven—making it dangerous to function in society without paying homage to heathen gods. Cultural ties and economic loyalties chained people to a multi-god system they could not break. Devotion to one God, Yahweh, often meant a decision to accept a martyr's death.

Yet amazingly so, first-century Christianity was able to stand against all of that. The early church's greatest achievement was its ability to trust the Holy Spirit to do His work. It meant the difference between success and failure. Conditions for the survival of New Testament church life have never changed.

Each generation of believers would do well to ask what kept the early church moving in the right direction to fulfill its mission. Discovering that secret will do much to permit local expressions of the body of Christ to do the same.

Safeguards Against Future Deception

God's Self-revelation: Disciples must always remember that God is committed to personally call the church together and sustain it through His own Self-revelation. Hebrews 1:1-4 confirms this fact by saying:

"God, after He spoke long ago to the fathers in the prophets in . . . many ways, in these last days has spoken to us in His Son, whom He appointed heir of all things, through whom also He made the world.

"And He is the radiance of His glory and the exact representation of His nature, and upholds all things by the word of His power. When He had made purification of sins, He sat down at the right hand of the Majesty on high; having become as much better than the angels, as He has inherited a more excellent name than they" (NASB).

God is personally and actively bringing forth the Church (*ekklēsia*) as the expression of the body of Christ. He never abandons His work *solely* to the leadership of

His delegated authorities on earth. On the contrary, He "upholds all things by the word of His power."

In each generation, the disciple's faith-response to God is based on a personal encounter with Him (John 1:12-13). The mystery of God is like an "unveiling" of His person as a believer personally experiences the indwelling presence of Jesus Christ.

All disciples in the body of Christ will do well to keep this scriptural guideline before them. God personally takes hold of each believer, causing him to desire to worship, and overseeing his development as a disciple of Christ (Isa. 6:3-13).

It is this Self-revelation in the person of Jesus Christ that stands as the foundation upon which individuals are called out of the "domain of darkness, and transferred . . . to the kingdom of His beloved Son" (Col. 1:13 NASB). God does not share this role with anyone outside the Godhead. He only delegates responsibility to undershepherds who are permitted to lead His disciples into maturity.

First John 2:22 says, "Who is the liar but the one who denies that Jesus is the Christ? This is the antichrist (*antichristos*), the one who denies the Father and the Son" (NASB).

"Anti" can mean "to be substituted for" or it can mean "to be in opposition to." In either case, it is the picture of a teacher who moves the disciple away from direct and personal communion with God through Jesus Christ.

A substitution takes place. The disciple develops a greater dependence upon the teacher or the "truth" than he does the Lord Jesus Christ. Idealistic teachers—ever zealous to serve God—must be careful never to invade the sovereign relationship each disciple should maintain with

Jesus Christ.

Fellowship (Koinōnia) *of the Holy Spirit:* Paul wrote, "The grace of the Lord Jesus Christ, and the love of God, and the fellowship (*koinōnia*) of the Holy Spirit, be with you all (2 Cor. 13:14 NASB). Paul stressed the importance of *koinōnia* by placing it alongside grace and love.

Just as the trinitarian personality cannot be separated, neither can the love of God, the grace of the Lord Jesus Christ and the *koinōnia* of the Holy Spirit. *Koinōnia* is more than the development of relationships between God's children. It is the life-flow of the Spirit of Jesus in each disciple, which actually makes the development of relationships possible.

The disciple does not establish relationships in order to find fellowship. He permits the fellowship which already exists in the Trinity to flow into his life and out to others. Thus, the *koinōnia* becomes the life-flow of relationships between all members of the body of Christ.

The disciple must remember that *koinōnia* is never discovered by "working out relationships" with the brethren. The reverse is actually true. Relationships with the brethren are established by walking in *koinōnia* with the Father. His life flowing through a disciple establishes balanced relationships within any local expression of the body of Christ.

God's Established Covenant: Covenant in the Old Testament is the Hebrew word *berith* which occurs 286 times. The LXX (Septuagint, or Greek translation made by early Jewish leaders of the Old Testament) translates *berith* as *diathēkē* 270 of the 286 times. *Diathēkē* is also used in the Greek New Testament for "covenant."

Fulfillment of covenant agreements are described in

the last will and testament of one who has died (Heb. 9:16-18). The deceased leaves his inheritance to a second party. The conditions of that last will and testament can not be changed after the person making it has died.

Hebrews 7:22 declares that Jesus became the "guarantee of a better covenant." All the conditions of the new covenant are met in the redemptive work of Jesus Christ. Nothing can be done by man to add to or take from the covenant God has established in Jesus Christ.

Jesus "once for all . . . offered up Himself" (Heb. 7:27 NASB) completing all the conditions of the new covenant. Yahweh's cutting of the covenant with Abraham (Gen. 15:17-18, Gen. 17:1-7) is already completed in Jesus Christ. The Lord passed between the two parts of the animal like a "smoking fire pot and flaming torch" binding himself to complete all conditions of the covenant. He has finalized the same at Calvary.

Extremes in discipleship can be avoided when believers remember there is no longer a need for covenant to be established. Once a disciple determines he cannot "establish covenant relationships" with others by his actions, he can then begin to interpret the covenant God has made with man and learn to walk in it.

Each believer is in covenant relationship with every other follower of Jesus Christ throughout the world. The practicality of such covenant relationships will only be understood as a disciple is obedient to walk out conditions of God's covenant with brethren he personally knows.

Any person who has a personal, redemptive relationship with Jesus Christ is a covenant brother or sister, whether he or she acknowledges it or not. Understanding the finality of God's covenant with all who enter it is a safeguard against extremes in covenant relationships.

Clarity of Committed Relationships: "Commit" is a word used repeatedly in the Scriptures to describe action to do either evil or good. Clarifying concepts of commitment within the body of Christ is a strong safeguard against extremes.

One extreme is that of the loner who says he believes in Jesus but will not demonstrate commitment to anyone. The other extreme is that of the disciple who will only declare commitment to a small band of believers.

Balance in committed relationships is encouraged when the disciple understands three facts about commitment. First, commitment is commanded by the Lord. Romans 12:1 exhorts to "present your bodies, a living and holy sacrifice, acceptable to God" (NASB). First John 3:23 says, "And this is His commandment, that we believe in the name of His Son Jesus Christ, and love one another, just as He commanded us" (NASB).

Second, commitment is all-inclusive. In 1 Corinthians 1:2, Paul addressed himself to "the church of God which is at Corinth, to those who have been sanctified in Christ Jesus, saints by calling, with all who in every place call upon the name of our Lord Jesus Christ, their Lord and ours" (NASB). It is the "all-inclusive" attitude in the disciple which permits him to define commitments in the local body of Christ without developing an "exclusive" or "elite" attitude about his church.

Third, commitment is practical. Although disciples are in covenant with all believers, practical application of committed relationships with all believers throughout the world is impossible. One can only walk out practical relationships with a few people. Yet it is the balance between "all-inclusive" commitment and "practical commitment" which allows the disciple to love the brethren.

When these three points are understood, the disciple is able to walk in a balance of submission and authority. He understands the practicality of submission of believers to each other. Yet he is able to respect those whom God has delegated leadership in the church. And he is also able to exercise delegated authority without abusing it.

Jesus said, "You know that the rulers of the Gentiles lord it over them, and their great men exercise authority over them. It is not so among you, but whoever wishes to become great among you shall be your servant, and whoever wishes to be first among you shall be your slave; just as the Son of Man did not come to be served, but to serve, and to give His life a ransom for many" (Matt. 20:25-28 NASB).

Dealing with Extremes

Most movements in Church history which became vulnerable to error were built on the unilateral submission of disciples to one person. That person may have said he was in a position to be corrected by others but his group's actions revealed otherwise.

In most cases, the leader asked for and received unconditional authority over his disciples. This "right" to exercise control over the will and conscience of his disciples made it nearly impossible for these followers to detect error in their leader.

The corporate ministry, both local and extra-local, are safeguards against such deception. According to Paul

(Acts 20:30), deception in the Ephesian church would begin when men pulled disciples out from under plural oversight of elders. The best safety, then, is still the life and authority within the local body of Christ—worked out in a balanced and practical manner.

According to Ecclesiastes 4:9, "Two are better than one because they have a good return for their labor" (NASB). In verse 12, the writer continued, "A cord of three strands is not quickly torn apart" (NASB).

Jesus established "two or three" as the basic unit for the church (Matt. 18:20). The church grew under the Holy Spirit's direction with a great company of disciples "of good report" and "full of the Holy Spirit and wisdom." Yet, the disciples did not arrive at such balance without having to struggle with extremes themselves.

According to Matthew 16:22 and Mark 8:31-33, Peter rebuked Jesus, trying to tell the Lord what He could and could not do about the crucifixion. Jesus, using strong words, pointed out to Peter that his thoughts were influenced by Satan. He had to learn how to stay in the will of God.

In Luke 10:17-20, the seventy disciples returned enamored with the power they discovered in casting out demons. Jesus gave them authority to cast out demons, but He also issued a firm warning about preoccupation with the ministry of deliverance. He told the seventy they should direct their thoughts to their own salvation as recorded in the Book of Life.

In Mark 9:33-37, the disciples slipped into a dispute over their own greatness. Each was sharing extreme thoughts about his ambitions. "I am the greatest disciple in the kingdom of heaven," declared each disciple. Jesus perceived the thought of their hearts (Luke 9:47) and dealt with the extreme by teaching them to serve one another.

Jesus faced a similar situation when the mother of James and John, the sons of Zebedee, came asking for her sons to be seated on the Lord's left and right in the kingdom of heaven. Honor is based on the ability to die, Jesus taught. It is not where one sits in God's kingdom.

Coming Out of Extremes

The apostle Paul recognized it was a difficult chore for some to come out of extremes. He found it hard to face the rebukes and antagonisms of people in extreme. In 2 Corinthians 2:3-4, he wrote, "And this is the very thing I wrote you, lest, when I came, I should have sorrow from those who ought to make me rejoice; having confidence in you all, that my joy would be the joy of you all.

"For out of much affliction and anguish of heart I wrote to you with many tears; not that you should be made sorrowful, but that you might know the love which I have especially for you" (NASB).

Walter R. Martin in *The Kingdom of the Cults* points out that a person in extreme has usually lived in isolation with his beliefs. It is difficult then for him to honestly face the possibility of error in his belief. The ability to admit any personal failure over his doctrine is impaired.[1]

Biblically, the first man to ever move away from balanced communion with God was Adam. Throughout Scripture, God makes it clear that He expects man to move from the error of his ways, both by his actions and by verbalizing his mistakes. "Turn from your wicked ways" and "confess your faults" are expressions of God's

[1]Walter R. Martin, *The Kingdom of the Cults*, (Minneapolis: Bethany Fellowship, Inc., 1970) p. 26.

guidance for a person who is ready to return to balance in the body of Christ.

The Word of God then offers definite guidelines to a person who recognizes the error in his life and desires to return to balance. *I have found seven steps a person can take in moving out of extreme.*

First, *make a decision to come out.* When Moses wanted to restore balance to the work of the Lord, he said, "Dedicate yourselves today to the Lord—for every man has been against his son and against his brother—in order that He may bestow a blessing upon you today" (Exod. 32:29 NASB). Joshua issued a similar call saying, "Choose you this day whom ye will serve" (Josh. 24:15).

Most people who move into extreme have made a decision which leads them into it. Leaders who guide others into extreme usually begin by asking their disciples to make a commitment to them personally. They bind disciples to themselves with cords that are difficult to break.

God gave the directive on breaking unhealthy covenant bonds in Deuteronomy 30:19-20. He declared, "I call heaven and earth to witness against you today, that I have set before you life and death, the blessing and the curse. So *choose* life in order that you may live, you and your descendants, by loving the Lord your God, by obeying His voice, and by holding fast to Him . . ." (NASB, italics mine).

Unhealthy bonds are then broken by renouncing the commitments which lead a man into them and returning to obey the Word of the Lord.

Charismatic teacher Gerald Derstine confronted extremes twice during the early days of his ministry, before the Lord raised him into prominence as a Bible teacher. The first instance came when he confronted the heavy authority of the bishops of the Mennonite church.

When the bishops stated Derstine's experience of receiving the Holy Spirit with the manifestation of charismatic gifts was unacceptable, he decided to disobey the bishops and obey the Holy Spirit. Six months later, Derstine found himself in a similar predicament—only this time, he was in Louisiana under the bondage of a prophet who was controlling his life.

Derstine had believed the prophet at first when the man told him everything God had said in the seven-day visitation of the Holy Spirit upon his Mennonite congregation in Minnesota. "When he told me everything God had said," Derstine recalled, "I accepted him as a prophet of God. No one knew at that time what had happened during those seven days except those believers who were in the meeting."

As the prophet directed more and foreboding commands to people, Derstine became uneasy in his spirit. The prophet had just told him God commanded Derstine to never shave or cut his hair again. Neither could he wear a white shirt. He was told to wear a flannel shirt the rest of his life. For his obedience, God was going to anoint Derstine's ministry greater than Elijah's.

"You're rebellious and disobedient to God," Derstine was told when he challenged the prophet over the directive prophecies. At that point, he decided to leave and return to Florida. "God will kill you and your family before you get out of town," the prophet declared. "You must stay here and obey the word of the Lord."

But Derstine's mind was set. "I decided I'd rather let God kill me than stay under the domination of that false prophet," he said. "I had a two weeks' growth of beard and wore a flannel shirt and with great fear I drove out of Louisiana waiting to see if God was going to kill us all."

Arriving safely in Sarasota, Florida, Derstine was still dressed according to the prophet's demands. "Feeling greatly condemned and afraid, I decided to go another step and shave," he said. "When nothing disastrous happened, I took off the flannel shirt.

"It was only then," he said, "when I decided to obey the Holy Spirit and search the Bible for truth, that the anointing came on my ministry. It has been on us ever since."

The best signal that a person is under bondage to extremism is the condemnation a leader might use when a disciple threatens to leave. One high-ranking leader of heavy submission teaching did just that to a departing disciple. "You will lose your place in the kingdom of God," the leader stated. "You will never again have authority with God and you will never be financially successful."

The believer who desires to leave extremism most likely will face such condemnation. Yet it is the decision to obey God and not man that brings release to a believer's spirit. Such a decision must be made when faith and practice conflict with Holy Scripture.

Second, *establish contact with balanced Christian leaders*. Dialogue and fellowship with mature Christian leaders who are in scriptural balance must follow the decision to leave extremism. These leaders will be able to provide support to a disciple while he adjusts his life.

When the prodigal son made his decision to leave the error he had moved into, his next step was to return to his father's house. The maturity of his father made him the best person to lovingly rehabilitate the prodigal to normal Christian living.

Third, *invite Christian brothers to help you understand your error.* The disciple who steps out of extreme teachings generally comes out bruised and confused. He has lost confidence in his own ability to detect heresy before it grips him. Without fellowship with mature Christians who can help interpret what happened, the wounded disciple often flounders.

Sometimes such people reject balanced Christianity all together. Other times they are fearful of anything that smacks of authority—even though it is balanced and limited under the delegated authority of the Lord.

Such was the case of a couple who visited our church. They had attached themselves to a Bible teacher who later went into extreme. Yet after they left him, they struggled with a fear of trusting anyone with the formation of their Christian lives.

Rather than returning to a balanced Christian atmosphere where they could understand how they fell into error, they floated from place to place trying to find the "right" fellowship—without success. Such action only increased their instability as effective Christians.

Fourth, *confirm all teachings of the Bible with your own study of Scripture.* That was the case of students at Berea according to Acts 17:11. "Now these were more noble-minded than those in Thessalonica, for they received the word with great eagerness, examining the Scriptures daily, to see whether these things were so" (NASB).

In 2 Timothy 3:16-17, Paul wrote, "All Scripture is inspired by God and profitable for teaching, for reproof, for training in righteousness; that the man of God may be adequate, equipped for every good work" (NASB).

If what a disciple is being taught is the Word of God, it will stand up under his efforts to understand it. The teacher who delivers it will not be threatened when a disciple insists that the teaching be tested in the light of other Scripture and by the testimony of other brothers.

Fifth, *admit the error to a band of responsible men.* Barnabas understood the importance of this step in restoring a man to balanced fellowship with the brethren. Acts 9:26 noted that the apostles were afraid of Paul even after his conversion. They remembered his previous extremes that had led to Stephen's death. They did not believe he was a true disciple of Jesus.

Then Barnabas took over. He "took hold of him and brought him to the apostles and described to them how he had seen the Lord on the road, and that He had talked to him, and how at Damascus he had spoken out boldly in the name of Jesus" (Acts 9:27 NASB).

Later, when Barnabas became the first pastor at Antioch (Acts 11:22), he sent for Paul to assist him. Paul worked beside Barnabas for a whole year. The relationship confirmed his place in the body of Christ (Acts 11:22-26, Acts 13:2-4).

Sixth, *return to active participation in a balanced Christian community.* The tendency of a disciple coming out of extreme is to reject anything that sounds like the teaching that led him astray. "The teaching we received appealed to young men, many of whom were quite inexperienced in living," said one group of men who left heavy submission teaching in shepherdship.

"Such men often tended to see life in idealistic,

black-and-white terms," the group continued. "Therefore they also saw authority in black-and-white terms and far too often were too inexperienced to handle it properly. The need to move into a clearly defined authority structure sometimes forced us to give men responsibility which they were not ready for. We now feel this is a big mistake."

One brother who came out of extreme teaching on submission was afraid to participate in Christian fellowship again. He felt others looked at him as a failure. It was only when he returned to fellowship with the brethren that his confidence began to return. His confidence did not return overnight. But support from the Christian community slowly restored him to a balanced position in the body of Christ.

Seventh, *make a new, balanced commitment to the lordship of Jesus Christ and to the brethren in the body of Christ.* Commitment is vital to the disciple's life. Paul declared, "I urge you therefore, brethren, by the mercies of God, to present your bodies a living and holy sacrifice, acceptable to God, which is your spiritual service of worship.

"And do not be conformed to this world, but be transformed by the renewing of your mind, that you may prove what the will of God is, that which is good and acceptable and perfect" (Rom. 12:1-2 NASB).

Remembering that the Lord does call people into community as He redeems them, disciples are then able to return to a commitment to Him and the community of believers. Heavy commitments to individual men can make believers afraid to enter into commitment with brethren again. However, balanced commitment will permit the Lord to restore a disciple to his place within the body of Christ.

Receiving a Brother Out of Extreme

"Brethren, even if a man is caught in any trespass, you who are spiritual, restore such a one in a spirit of gentleness; looking to yourself, lest you too be tempted" (Gal. 6:1 NASB). Paul exhorted the church at Galatia to remember that any one of them could have fallen into extreme. Such a thought permitted them to gently receive back a fallen brother.

Brethren who have the responsibility of restoring a brother into fellowship must remember he is a bruised reed who has lost confidence in himself, in his fellowmen—and often in God. His spirit is already bruised by heaviness and condemnation; he will not be able to handle more when he returns.

James noted that receiving a brother back from extreme error was a calling from God. "My brethren, if any among you strays from the truth, and one turns him back, let him know that he who turns a sinner from the error of his way will save his soul from death, and will cover a multitude of sins" (James 5:19-20 NASB).

Willingness on the part of the brethren to be used in such a manner carries with it the redemptive healing power of the Lord Jesus Christ.

When Paul recognized there was a leader in Corinth who had repented from leading disciples astray, he wrote, "But if any has caused sorrow, he has caused sorrow not to me, but to some degree—in order not to say too much—to all of you. Sufficient for such a one is this punishment which was inflicted by the majority, so that on the contrary you should rather forgive and comfort him, lest somehow such a one be overwhelmed by excessive sorrow. Wherefore I urge you to reaffirm your love for him" (2 Cor. 2:5-8 NASB).

In these verses, Paul gave four guidelines for restoring a brother into fellowship who had caused the extreme. Such advice will restore both the leader of the extreme and his disciples—when they are ready to return to balance.

First, *remember that the agony he suffers of knowing he went into extreme is enough punishment*, (verse six). If the brother has reached the point he is ready to return to balance, let the pain he has suffered in facing up to his error be enough. The brethren should do nothing to punish him for his mistakes.

Second, *forgive him for his mistake*, (verse seven). This action involves a deliberate and complete act of forgiveness on the part of the brethren. That is to say, they should begin conducting themselves toward the returning brother as if nothing had happened to rupture the fellowship within the body of Christ.

Third, *comfort the brother*, (verse seven). Paul listed this guideline because the returning brother often runs the risk of being "overwhelmed by excessive sorrow." Such an attitude often drives a repentant brother into seclusion. In extreme cases where people have left groups like the Children of God, some have actually contemplated suicide.

Said one man who came out of the COG movement, "It's hard to look back on five and a half years of your life and not find something there that was good. I still feel very close to those whom I knew in the group. All in all, I thank God I can offer reassurance to the victims and families of these cults, not as an outsider but as one who has been there. Not as one condemning but as one forgiven."

Fourth, *reaffirm love to the brother*, (verse eight). Such an affirmation of love is essential in the Christian community. It is the nature of God to give love to a person coming out of error.

When the prodigal son returned home he came saying, "Father, I have sinned against heaven and in your sight; I am no longer worthy to be called your son" (Luke 15:21 NASB), the father received him with loving, opened arms.

Explaining why he had received the prodigal in such a way, the father said to the older son, "But we had to be merry and rejoice, for this brother of yours was dead and has begun to live, and was lost and has been found" (Luke 15:32 NASB).

The prodigal's life away from his father's house was costly—yet it taught him where genuine life was found. It was at father's house. Before leaving, he struggled to find his place in life. After testing the futility of living in extremes, he recognized where to find his place. It was at father's house in fellowship with his brethren.

The place for every disciple of Jesus Christ is no different today. "In My Father's house are many dwelling places," declared Jesus (John 14:2 NASB). Father's house is the only secure place for a disciple of Jesus. That, to me, is a balanced local body of believers.